ERASING YOUR CRIMINAL BACKGROUND LEGALLY

The Ultimate Guide to Second Chances

By Daniel Hall, Esq.

with Sarah Greenberg, Esq.

Legal Research Editor:
Konstantin Parkhomenko, Esq.

Erasing Your Criminal Background Legally
The Ultimate Guide to Second Chances

ISBN: 143824892X
EAN-13: 9781438248929

"This document is designed to provide accurate and authoritative information in regard to the subject matter covered. It is provided with the understanding that the author/publisher is not engaged in rendering legal, accounting or other professional services. If legal advice or expert assistance is required, the services of a competent professional should be sought." —
From a declaration of Principles, jointly adopted by a Committee of the American Bar Association and a Committee of Publishers.

DISCLAIMER

DEDICATION

To my creator who, thankfully,
is the God of Second Chances.

~ Daniel Hall

I want to thank my family for
their ever-present love and
support, God, and Second Chances.

~ Sarah Greenberg

MORE RAVE REVIEWS FOR THIS BOOK

This book is a terrific guide to understanding the criminal expunction process and provides practical tips regarding the possibility of obtaining legal representation to attempt to have a minor criminal offense or offenses expunged from a person's record. Such an undertaking could make a big difference with many types of licensing authorities. In my former role as a law school associate dean, I would frequently encounter students who had been convicted of minor offenses while juveniles or during their college years. Often, they would have been advised that their records could be expunged, but they had never followed up. Most lawyers know little to nothing about this process, and this book fills a needed gap in the legal literature.

Brian D. Shannon
    Charles "Tex" Thornton Professor of Law
    Texas Tech University, School of Law

***

Texas outlawed the branding of men in the 1800's. A criminal arrest now serves as an electronic tattoo on the forehead of the citizen accused. This guide is THE starting place to heal a blemished past.

Gerald Rogen, Esq.
    Past-president of the Coastal Bend Criminal Defense Lawyers Association

I have mediated thousands of cases and I know how difficult it is the put a life back together after a mistake – especially a mistake that resulted in an arrest. If you're haunted by misjudgments or youthful indiscretions that led to a criminal record wipe them clean with help from this book!

Andrew Lehrman, Esq.
  Mediator & Past-president of the Nueces County Bar Association

***

"Erasing Your Criminal Background Legally" is a great start to getting your life back together. Hall has done a superb job of gathering in one book the laws of the fifty states to help you figure out where to start. As an attorney who practices in this area, I found Hall's research to be invaluable.

Michael Dezsi, Esq.
  Successful representation of Geoffrey Fieger & plaintiff counsel in lawsuits against Former United States Attorney General Alberto Gonzalez after his clients were harassed & investigated for supporting the 2004 presidential campaign of John Edwards

***

"Every lawyer who has thought about helping a client secure a second chance will find this unique book very useful. Lawyers, law firms, and law libraries will want to have this reference book readily available."

Alison G. Myhra
  Professor of Law, Texas Tech University, School of Law

Table of Contents

ACKNOWLEDGEMENTS

I wish to acknowledge my wonderful wife, Lanette, who loved the idea of this book from the start and who kept reminding me to keep working on it even in the face of countless other projects... without her the book may never have been finished.

I wish to thank my local WestLaw representative who helped me in the early research phase.

I also wish to send out a HUGE thank you to my co-author Sarah Greenberg; she is a big reason the book is as thorough and well written as it is.

I also wish to thank and acknowledge the following people listed in no particular order: Gerald Rogen, Esq., Robert Breitzmann, Mimi, my clients who needed an expungement (they showed me how much this book was needed); Congressman Charles D. Rangel for his leadership with the "Second Chance for Ex-Offenders Act", and all the people who helped me edit this book including Konstantin Parkhomenko (our crack legal research editor who rose to every occasion and did a truly superlative job!), Cheryl Aplin, Wendy Perez, and especially Michelle Ostrye (Michelle's editing advice helped me get on Law Review back in law school for which I will always be grateful and she has done a truly wonderful job editing this book), and my book designer Chiquitta Harris.

~ Daniel Hall

AUTHOR'S INTRODUCTION

Have you been a perfect angel your whole life? *(I can see you adjusting your halo.)*

Many of us have suffered from a momentary lapse in good judgment that resulted in an arrest. Pinched!

Unfortunately, while criminal charges may have gone nowhere, the arrest record may still trip you up.

What do I mean?

Have you ever had to answer a question on a job or license application like: "Have you ever been arrested?"

See? This can get sticky. You don't want to lie but you really would rather not answer the question either.

Alas, there is hope.

There is a little-known and little-used procedure in most jurisdictions in the United States that allows, in appropriate circumstances, for a total erasure of an arrest record. Additionally, even if you can't qualify for a total erasure of your background, there may be legal ways to hide your background so that at least it will not be easily discoverable by an over-zealous potential employer.

As a licensed attorney, I have used similar legal remedies to assist clients with erasing or hiding of arrests and/or convictions for minor offenses. The difference it has made in their lives amazes me. For example, I have seen military careers blossom, professional licenses granted, and overseas employment gained all because I was able to help tidy up minor criminal blemishes in the lives of otherwise upstanding and law-abiding citizens.

What I am saying is there may be a way for you to chase off the skeletons in your closet that have long haunted you. The law in many U.S. jurisdictions recognizes the need to grant clean slates and second chances. I don't know whether you qualify. I don't know your circumstances. All I am trying to say is "open your mind to the possibility." That is what this book is all about: showing you the possibilities.

The good results I've seen and the apparent lack of wide-spread public knowledge prompted me to write this book.

This book is designed to help those people with petty criminal records. And make no mistake—this is a large group. Indeed, CBS News "Eye on America" reported that as many as one person in seven has some sort of criminal record.

If you're one of them, use this book to find out whether you qualify for an expungement or some other remedy in the jurisdiction where you were arrested.

How to use this book

This book is intended to summarize and analyze the criminal erasure (expungement) laws of each jurisdiction within the United States and is organized by state or territory. Your job is simply to find and read the entry for the jurisdiction in which you were arrested. The information is designed to help you learn whether the circumstances of your arrest are expugnable. Having said that, even if it does not at first appear that you are eligible I would still recommend seeking the opinion of a lawyer competent in obtaining expungements. You see, laws change and what was once impossible may now be possible and vice versa. So action is imperative and time may be of the essence. Thus, I describe how to find such a competent attorney in the last chapter of this book.

A word of caution

This book is not a do-it-yourself manual. Don't try to use this book to clean up your own record. Instead, use it to explore the possibilities. If you find that you may qualify for expungement, then contact a competent attorney in the state where you were arrested.

Now get started. I wish you the best of luck.

Daniel Hall
Corpus Christi, Texas

ALABAMA

Introduction

In Alabama, the statutes governing expungement of criminal records are unclear and often lead to inconsistent results. No statute expressly grants Alabama courts the power to expunge criminal records. Judges do, however, issue orders of expungement from time to time, and the availability of expungement may depend solely on which court hears the case. This fact is potentially good news for someone in a close call situation because, without a clear statutory framework, Alabama judges arguably have more latitude to use personal discretion in deciding whether an applicant is worthy of an expungement.

The Law in Alabama

Alabama Code Section 41-9-625 provides the mechanism for gathering data such as photographs and fingerprints of people arrested in the state. All of this information is stored in the Alabama Criminal Justice Information Computer System (ACJIS). The Code does not specify how to petition a court for expungement of these records, but it does provide that if a person is arrested and later released without charge or is cleared of the offense, all records of that offense stored in the ACJIS are to be eliminated within thirty days.

Alabama Code Section 41-9-645 contains provisions which allow an individual to challenge information in their criminal record. Lawyers successfully have relied on such statutes from time to time to secure an expungement order for their clients. It is summarized below.

> If an individual believes that information in his or her criminal record is inaccurate or incomplete, he or she may request the original agency that had control of the records to purge, modify, or supplement it.

> If the agency refuses to act, the individual may appeal the agency's decision to the circuit court in his or her county within thirty days of the agency's decision. The individual must send notice to the agency by registered mail that an appeal has been entered.

Alabama Code Section 41-6-646 grants the court the power to order a criminal record purged, modified, or supplemented if the record is found to be incomplete, inaccurate, or misleading.

Alabama Code Section 45-8-82.40 establishes a "pretrial diversionary program." This program allows the district attorney to move cases out of the criminal justice system after weighing certain factors including the cost of prosecution and the nature of the offense. Individuals charged with certain types of criminal offenses, however, are not eligible to participate in the program. If the district attorney and advisory committee allow an individual to participate, the district attorney will impose certain conditions of behavior and conduct on the individual for a specified period of time. After the individual has satisfactorily completed the program, he or she may ask the district attorney to file a petition seeking to expunge the records.

Expungement for Juveniles

Like most states, Alabama makes it easier for juveniles to expunge their criminal records. In fact, the Attorney General of Alabama has indicated, despite several adult expungement orders to the contrary, that juvenile records are the only criminal records that a court may order expunged. Alabama Code Section 12-15-136 provides the authority and procedure for the expungement or sealing of juvenile records. The statute is summarized below.

The court on its own motion or on the motion of an individual who was the subject of a delinquency proceeding may vacate its order and seal the criminal records if it finds that:

1. Two years have passed since the final release of the individual from custody or supervision; and

2. The individual has not been convicted of a felony or misdemeanor involving moral turpitude, nor adjudicated delinquent in those two years, and there are no such charges pending.

Any adjudication of delinquency or felony conviction after the records are sealed automatically unseals the records.

An individual may file a motion with the court requesting that all of his or her juvenile records be destroyed five years after reaching age of majority.

Upon entry of sealing or destruction order, a case shall be treated as if it never occurred. The individual subject to the order may state he or she has never been arrested or convicted of the offense subject to the order.

Eligibility

For adults, The Alabama Code concerning expungement is very unclear and sets forth only general circumstances under which criminal records may be changed. Under Code Section 41-9-645, anyone may petition the court to have his or her criminal record purged, modified, or supplemented if he or she believes the information contained within it is inaccurate or incomplete, but the likelihood of obtaining an order of expungement depends on whether the court feels it can, by its own authority, grant one in the absence of specific statutory authority.

Effect of Expungement

Upon the entry of the order, the proceedings in the case shall be sealed. As stated above, the juvenile court, in its discretion, may by special order in an individual case permit inspection by or release of information in the records to any clinic, hospital, or agency which has the person under care. Also, any later conviction for felony charges involving sexual offenses, drugs, weapons, or violence, or threats of violence will cause the earlier sealing order to be nullified.

Be that as it may, Alabama still has on its books §12-15-137. Proceedings for destruction of legal and social files and records of juvenile courts pertaining to certain persons and effect thereof which provide that a person who has been the subject of a delinquency petition and has met the following condition –

A youthful offender does not have any felony or misdemeanor charges involving sexual offenses, drugs, weapons, or violence, or threats of violence in those two years, and there are no such charges pending.

That person within five years after reaching the age of majority may file a motion requesting the destruction of all records pertaining to his or her case. If the juvenile court grants the motion, copies of the order shall be sent to all offices, departments, or agencies that are repositories of the records, and all the offices, departments, and agencies shall comply with the order.

The effect of expungement of an adult criminal record is uncertain. The statute provides that the court may require the record purged, but this term is not defined in the code. Due to the absence of clear statutory language, the consequences of expungement are hard to determine.

Other Remedies

An individual convicted of a criminal offense in the State of Alabama may apply for a restoration of voting rights or a full pardon by contacting the Pardon Unit of the Alabama Board of Pardons and Paroles. Certain information must be contained in the pardon request. Once the Board receives an application, it will conduct an investigation and hearing to determine whether to grant the pardon.

The Pardon Unit contact information:

(334) 242- 8700
The Board of Pardons and Paroles
P.O. Box 302405
Montgomery, AL 36130

Conclusion

While the Alabama Code provides that an individual may petition to have his or her arrest records purged or modified if they believe the records to be inaccurate or incomplete, the ability to obtain expungement depends on the policy views of the court and the authority to grant expungement must be effectively argued.

As we have said multiple times throughout this book "DO NOT TRY THIS AT HOME." There are numerous pitfalls and perils for those trying to obtain an expungement on their own without the help of an attorney. We've said it before and we'll say it now, ***do not** try a "do-it-yourself expungement."*

The primary problem is "do it yourselfers" can stir up a long dormant and as of yet un-pursued case. In other words, if you go making haphazard inquiries in the wrong case you can arouse prosecutorial interest and fire up an investigation of you and your case/arrest. Thus, use the resource section of our website at www.ultimatesecondchance.com/resources to help find an attorney in your area.

ALASKA

Introduction

In Alaska, no statute explicitly grants the right to expungement, and Alaskan courts have not definitively answered the question whether or not they have the inherent power to expunge criminal records. Alaska statutes do contain a provision that allows for the sealing of criminal records that closely parallels the expungement statutes of other states. Another statute, Alaska's set aside statute, may also provide some relief from the haunting effects of a criminal record. Some confusion exists as to the relationship between these two statutes and their effect on criminal records, which I attempt to clarify in this section.

The Law in Alaska

Section 12.62.180 of the Alaska Statutes, entitled "Sealing of Criminal Justice Information," closely parallels the expungement statutes of other jurisdictions. It provides the possibility of sealing criminal information but only in the case where the arrest or conviction arose due to mistaken identity or false accusation. The statute is summarized below.

An individual may submit a written request to the agency responsible for maintaining criminal records, asking it to seal information that resulted from mistaken identity or false accusation. If the decision is unfavorable, the individual may appeal the agency's decision to the proper court, but the individual has the burden of proving the decision was clearly mistaken.

Eligibility

The Alaska statute concerning the sealing of records is extremely vague. It allows for the sealing of records only in the event the information was obtained due to mistaken identity or false accusation. Other than this general, preliminary requirement, the statute makes no distinction between types of offenses, whether felony, misdemeanor, DWI or DUI that may be sealed. Also, the statute makes no distinction between the ability to seal information concerning minors and information concerning adults.

Thus, the fact that the statute is vague can be a good thing if your situation falls within a gray area. That is to say, with well-defined statutes and clear eligibility requirements a person either will or will not fit the criteria. When, as with the Alaska statute, there is statutory ambiguity, the door is potentially open to a wider cross-section of cases. Why? Because it is much more difficult for a court to determine who is eligible and who is not. It is in such circumstances where luck and good lawyering can help determine the outcome.

Effect of the Sealing of Records

An individual successful in sealing his or her records may deny the existence of an arrest, charge, conviction, or sentence shown in the information. The information is not destroyed, however, and may be provided to another person or agency for:

1. Managing records;

2. Possible criminal justice employment;

3. Review by the individual who is the subject of the information sealed;

4. Statistical and research purposes;

5. The necessary prevention of imminent harm to a person; and

6. Use authorized by a statute or court order

Other Remedies

Alaska's set-aside statute, (Section 12.55.085 of the Alaska Statutes) entitled "Suspending Imposition of Sentence" is meant to be a one-time opportunity for deserving first-time offenders, and it is not available for all offenses. After the successful completion of a probationary period, the court may discharge the offender without the imposition of a sentence and may issue a certificate to that effect.

The Alaska Supreme Court has held that the inherent power to expunge criminal records does not extend to defendants who receive suspended sentences and have their convictions set aside after successfully completing a probationary period. The court has not expressly announced that an inherent power to expunge criminal records exists, but rather, the court stated that if the power did exist, courts may exercise it only in the case of an innocent defendant.

Another alternative to expungement in Alaska is Executive Clemency provided in Article III, Section 21 of the Alaska Constitution. Executive Clemency is the Governor's power to grant pardons, commutations of sentences, remissions of fines and forfeitures, and amnesty. A full pardon relieves an offender from punishment and the disabilities imposed due to a conviction of a criminal offense. Anyone who has committed a crime under the laws of Alaska may apply for a pardon at anytime.

To begin the process of applying for a pardon, an applicant must first complete and submit an Eligibility Determination form to the Alaska Board of Parole office. These forms may be requested from the Board. If an applicant is found to be eligible, the Board will conduct an investigation and submit its findings to the Governor who makes the determination whether or not to grant a pardon.

Board of Parole contact information:

Alaska Board of Parole
ATTN: Clemency Determination
P.O. Box 112000
Juneau, AK 99811-2000

Conclusion

Because Alaska's statutory framework is ambiguous, there is more cause for hope for those who may have a more complicated (questionable) past. However, seek out the services of a competent lawyer to investigate whether there is a possibility of obtaining an expungement in a particular case.

Also, as we have said multiple times throughout this book "DO NOT TRY THIS AT HOME." There are numerous pitfalls and perils for those trying to obtain an expungement on their own without the help of an attorney. We've said it before and we'll say it now, ***do not* try a "do it yourself expungement."**

The primary problem is "do it yourselfers" can stir up a long dormant and as of yet un-pursued case. In other words, if you go making haphazard inquiries in the wrong case you can arouse prosecutorial interest and fire up an investigation of you and your case/arrest. Thus, use the resource section of our website at www.ultimatesecondchance.com/resources to help find an attorney in your area.

ARIZONA

Introduction

Arizona, like many other states, does not have a clearly defined expungement law, but it does have a few different statutes that provide some relief from a criminal record. Specifically, depending on the final outcome of the case, an individual may petition for an Entry of Clearance on Records, or petition that the conviction be set aside. Neither of these two options destroys the criminal record entirely, and many times, in the case of a set-aside, the information contained in the records may be released for licensing and employment purposes.

The Law in Arizona

Section 13-4051 of the Arizona Criminal Code provides for an Entry of Clearance on Records, which means a notation is entered on the individual's criminal record that he or she has been cleared of the offense. This option is available only to individuals who are innocent and were wrongfully arrested or charged. The statute is summarized below.

> A. Anyone wrongfully arrested, indicted, or charged for a crime can petition the court to enter a notation that the individual has been cleared upon all records relating to the arrest or indictment.

B. The judge will conduct a hearing on the matter, and if he or she believes that an entry on the records is justified, he or she will issue an order requiring a notation that the individual has been cleared on the records.

C. The order prevents the records from being released to anyone unless the court orders it.

For individuals charged and convicted of a criminal offense, Section 13-907 of the Arizona Criminal Code might provide some relief. This section allows the court to set aside a criminal offense once the individual charged with the offense has successfully completed a probationary period. The statute is summarized below.

A. Any person convicted of a criminal offense who successfully completes a probationary period and receives a discharge by the court, can apply to the judge who announced the sentence to have the judgment of guilt set aside.

B. If the judge grants the application, he or she will set aside the judgment of guilt and order that the person be released from the disabilities stemming from the conviction.

Expungement for Juveniles

Unlike the adult set-aside statute found in the Arizona Criminal Code, Section 13-921 is a set-aside statute for offenders under the age of 18 and it makes use of the word "expungement." The statute is summarized below.

A. A court may enter a judgment of guilt and put the juvenile offender on probation if all of the following apply:

1. The individual is under 18 years of age at the time of the offense;

2. It is a felony offense;

3. The individual is not sentenced to imprisonment; and

4. The individual does not have a prior felony conviction.

B. After the individual successfully completes probation, the court can set aside the judgment of guilt, dismiss the indictment, expunge the individual's record, and order he or she be released from all disabilities resulting from the conviction.

Eligibility

Only people who are factually innocent and were wrongfully arrested may obtain an Entry of Clearance on Records. The wrongfully arrested individual must prove to the court that no legal or factual basis for the charge existed. The Entry of Clearance on Records statute, though silent on the matter, seems to imply that anyone wrongfully arrested, regardless of the offense, may apply for such an entry.

On the other hand, individuals convicted of certain criminal offenses may petition a court to set aside the judgment of guilt. It is the judge's discretion alone whether such petition will be granted. If the judge determines setting aside the judgment is in the interest of justice, then he or she will grant the request. Certain criminal convictions will make a person ineligible for set-aside. Set-asides are not allowed for crimes involving:

1. The infliction of serious physical injury;

2. The use of a deadly weapon or instrument;

3. Sexual offenses; and,

5. Victims under 15 years of age

Effect of Expungement

The Arizona statutes are unclear as to the effect of expungement on a criminal record. What is clear is that the records are not destroyed or sealed and can be accessed under certain circumstances. For example, a court order may provide access to records subject to an Entry of Clearance. Gaining access to records subject to a set-aside may prove even easier. The courts have held that the expungement or set-aside of a criminal conviction does not protect an individual from having to disclose the fact that he or she has been convicted when directly asked. All convictions, even those that were set aside, are available for use in a later criminal proceeding against that individual.

Other Remedies

An individual convicted of a criminal offense in Arizona may file an application with the clerk of the superior court in which he or she was convicted for a Restoration of Civil Rights. The rights that may be restored vary, depending on the nature of the underlying offense, and can include anything from the right to serve on a jury, to the right to own a firearm in certain limited circumstances.

Conclusion

While the Arizona Criminal Code allows an eligible person to petition the court on his or her own behalf for the relief of set-aside or Entry of Clearance on Record, the process can be extremely complex. You must prove to the judge that setting aside a judgment of guilt is in the interest of justice, or in the case of an Entry of Clearance on Record, that absolutely no factual basis existed for arrest. An experienced and qualified attorney is better equipped to successfully prove such arguments.

As we have said multiple times throughout this book "DO NOT TRY THIS AT HOME." There are numerous pitfalls and perils for those trying to obtain an expungement on their own without the help of an attorney. We've said it before and we'll say it now, ***do not** try a "do-it-yourself expungement."*

The primary problem is "do it yourselfers" can stir up a long dormant and as of yet un-pursued case. In other words, if you go making haphazard inquiries in the wrong case you can arouse prosecutorial interest and fire up an investigation of you and your case/arrest. Thus, use the resource section of our website at www.ultimatesecondchance.com/resources to help find an attorney in your area.

ARKANSAS

Introduction

In Arkansas, the statutes are very clear regarding the availability of expungement. The Arkansas Code of Criminal Procedure defines the term "expungement," outlines the procedures and requirements necessary to apply for expungement, and details how an expungement affects a criminal record.

The Law in Arkansas

Sections 16-90-904 of the Arkansas Code of Criminal Procedure, entitled the "Expungement and Sealing of Criminal Records" cover the area of expungement. The statutes set forth clear guidelines for obtaining an expungement of a criminal record. The statutes are summarized below.

> An individual who was charged and arrested for a criminal offense but for whom the charges were later dismissed, or an individual was acquitted at trial, may file a uniform petition to seal records with the court in the county where the crime took place.

> The Arkansas Crime Information Center provides a uniform petition and order to seal

records all individuals must use and request a sealing of records. The petition must include:

1. A statement made under oath indicating whether the individual making the request has any felony charges pending;

2. A statement that the information contained in the petition is true and correct;

3. The individual's full name, race, sex, and date of birth;

4. The individual's full name at the time of arrest and conviction, if different from his or her current name;

5. The crimes for which the person was convicted and the date of conviction;

6. The name of the court which entered the conviction;

7. The provision under which the individual was sentenced that provides for sealing or expungement of the record; and

8. The specific records to be sealed.

A copy of the petition must be served upon the prosecuting authority for that county and the arresting agency. If either opposes the relief, the court may grant a hearing. If the court determines the records should be sealed, it will enter a uniform order that is filed with the clerk. The clerk will then sequester all of the records subject to the sealing order.

Eligibility

An individual who was charged and arrested for a criminal offense but for whom the charges were later dismissed, or the individual who was acquitted, is eligible to have his or her records relating to the case expunged. Arkansas also has developed a community punishment program establishing probationary periods for certain types of targeted criminal offenses. Those offenses include misdemeanors, DWIs, Class C or Class D felonies that are not violent or sexual, Class A and Class B controlled substance felonies, and all other unclassified felonies that are not violent or sexual. Upon the successful completion of the probationary period, the individual may apply to have the records sealed.

Effect of Expungement

An individual whose record has been expunged has all rights restored and is completely exonerated. The record that has been expunged does not affect any civil rights or liberties, unless specifically provided by law. The individual's offense is deemed as never having occurred, and the individual may state the offense never occurred and no records exist. The records in question are sealed, sequestered, and treated as confidential, but not physically destroyed. The records may be released if:

1. Requested by the individual whose records were sealed;

2. Requested by a criminal justice agency in conjunction with an application for employment with the agency by the person whose record was sealed;

3. Requested by a court because of a subsequent conviction; or

4. Requested by a prosecuting attorney in connection with the prosecution of another offense against that individual.

Expungement for Juveniles

Arkansas sets forth clear guidelines for the expungement of offenses committed as a minor. The statutes are summarized below.

A person convicted of a nonviolent felony under the age of 18 who was incarcerated or placed on probation, after completing the sentence or probation period, may petition the convicting court to have the record of the conviction expunged. If the court determines it is in the best interests of the individual and the state, it will enter an order expunging the record.

Any person who committed a felony while under the age of 16 years of age, was convicted and given a suspended sentence, later received a pardon, and has not been convicted of another criminal offense, is entitled to an order from the sentencing court expunging the criminal record.

Other Remedies

Article 6, Section 18 of the Arkansas Constitution entitled "Executive Clemency," grants the Governor the power to pardon any criminal offense other than treason or impeachment. Once an individual receives a pardon from the Governor, he or she is eligible for expungement and his or her criminal record will be sealed. A person requesting a pardon must first have his or her application screened by the Arkansas Board of Parole.

Arkansas Board of Parole contact information:

(501) 682-3850
Arkansas Board of Parole
P.O. Box 34085
Little Rock, AR 72203

Conclusion

While the statutes regarding expungement in Arkansas are rather clear and straightforward, the procedure involved is time consuming and chances of successfully obtaining a pardon or expungement improve greatly with the help of an experienced attorney.

As we have said multiple times throughout this book

"DO NOT TRY THIS AT HOME." There are numerous pitfalls and perils for those trying to obtain an expungement on their own without the help of an attorney. We've said it before and we'll say it now, ___do not___ *try a "do-it-yourself expungement."*

The primary problem is "do it yourselfers" can stir up a long dormant and as of yet un-pursued case. In other words, if you go making haphazard inquiries in the wrong case you can arouse prosecutorial interest and fire up an investigation of you and your case/arrest. Thus, use the resource section of our website at www.ultimatesecondchance.com/resources to help find an attorney in your area.

CALIFORNIA

Introduction

In California, statutes allowing the expungement of DNA samples and sealing of criminal records are clearly defined. The status governing sealing of records actually call for the eventual destruction of the criminal record in question, but the statutes apply only to those people the court finds to be factually innocent. The person requesting the sealing of records must prove to the court there was no reasonable cause for the arrest to establish factual innocence. In other circumstances, California allows for limited expungement for those with criminal convictions.

The Law in California

Section 851.8 of the California Penal Code allows for the sealing and destruction of arrest records upon a finding of factual innocence. The statute is summarized below.

When a person has been arrested but:

1. No charges were filed;

2. Charges were filed but there was no conviction; or

3. The person was acquitted,

That person may petition the law enforcement agency that arrested him or her to destroy the records of the arrest. A copy of the petition must be sent to the district attorney and upon a determination that the person is factually innocent; the records are for three years and then destroyed.

In the event the law enforcement agency denies the request, the individual may petition the superior court to seal the records. A copy of the petition to the court must be sent to the district attorney.

The individual requesting the sealing of records must show that no reasonable cause existed to believe that he or she committed the offense for which the arrest was made.

Eligibility

All persons believing themselves to be factually innocent of the offense for which he or she was arrested may apply to have his or her records sealed and destroyed, regardless of whether the offense is classified as a felony or misdemeanor. The Department of Justice provides the forms for the application process. The sealing of records does not apply to any offense classified as an "infraction."

Effect of the Sealing of Records

When a court grants a request to seal records, the court shall issue a written declaration that the person factually innocent is exonerated of the charges, and the records are to be permanently obliterated three years after the order. The arrest is considered not to have occurred and the individual does not have to disclose the fact that it ever took place. A finding of factual innocence is not admissible as evidence in any later actions.

Sealing of Records for Juveniles

Like many other states, California makes it easier for an individual to have his or her record sealed if he or she was convicted of a criminal offense as a juvenile. Section 781 of the California Welfare and Institutions Code pertaining to the sealing of juvenile records is very similar to the statute outlining the sealing of records for adults, except that a juvenile does not need to be found factually innocent to be eligible to have his or her records sealed. The statute is summarized below.

Anyone charged with a criminal offense as a juvenile may petition the court to seal his or her records five years or more after the case has terminated or anytime after reaching the age of 18.

If, after a hearing, the court finds that since the termination of the action, the person petitioning to have his or her records sealed has not been convicted of a felony or a misdemeanor involving moral turpitude, it shall order all records of the juvenile court sealed. The records may not be sealed for a juvenile charged with certain violent crimes listed under Section 707(b) of the California Welfare and Institutions Code after obtaining the age of 14. The sealing of juvenile records is not available for offenses under the Motor Vehicle Code.

If the court orders the person's records sealed, the arrest is treated as if it never occurred, and the person may reply accordingly to any questions about the events.

The court shall order the destruction of a person's juvenile records that are sealed five years after the entry of the order sealing the record.

Other Remedies

California provides very limited relief in the case of an adult who has been convicted of a criminal offense. Section 1203.4 of the California Penal Code sets out the steps an individual may take to obtain a certificate of rehabilitation or pardon. The statute is summarized below. Only in rare circumstances will the Governor consider anyone for a pardon who has not been discharged from probation or parole for at least ten years. There are two ways to apply for a pardon: by first obtaining a certificate of rehabilitation from the superior court as outlined below, or individuals ineligible for a certificate of rehabilitation may apply for a pardon directly from the Governor. The statute is summarized below.

> After the successful completion of a period of probation, an individual may pay a fee not to exceed $120 and apply in writing to the court to have the verdict of guilt set aside, and the court shall dismiss the defendant and release him or her from all penalties and disabilities resulting from the conviction. The court will then forward the certificate of rehabilitation to the Governor for pardon consideration.

> The conviction still may be used in later prosecutions against the individual, and the individual must disclose the conviction in response to any direct question contained in an application for public office, or for licensure by any government agency. The individual also is prohibited from purchasing or owning a firearm.

> This type of relief is not available for certain violations of the Vehicle Code and most misdemeanors. This relief also is not available for sexual offenses; however the Governor may pardon these types of offenses in extraordinary circumstances.

Most individuals with misdemeanor convictions are ineligible to apply for a certificate of rehabilitation through the court, but may apply directly to the Governor for a pardon. To obtain a pardon application you must make a written request to the office of the Governor.

Office of the Governor Contact Information:

Governor's Office
State Capitol
ATTN: Legal Affairs Secretary
Sacramento, CA 95814

Conclusion

California statutes provide that an individual may petition the court on his or her own behalf to have his or her records sealed or a guilty verdict set aside. There are, however, strict formalities and requirements that must be met in both instances, and as always, it is best to seek the advice of an experienced attorney.

As we have said multiple times throughout this book "DO NOT TRY THIS AT HOME." There are tons of pitfalls and perils for those trying to obtain an expunction on their own without the help of an attorney. We've said it before and we'll say it now, *do not try a "do it yourself expunction."*

The primary problem is "do it yourselfers" can stir up a long dormant and as of yet un-pursued case. In other words, if you go making haphazard inquiries in the wrong case you can arouse prosecutorial interest and fire up an investigation of you and your case/arrest. Thus, use the resource section of our website at www.ultimatesecondchance.com/resources to help find an attorney in your area.

COLORADO

Introduction

Colorado law allows for the sealing of records in certain adult cases as well as the expungement of records in certain juvenile cases. Like many states, Colorado provides these remedies under limited, narrowly, defined circumstances.

The Law in Colorado

Section 24-72-308 of the Colorado Government Code entitled "Sealing of Records," allows for expungement of criminal records in limited circumstances. The granting is entirely within the discretion of the court. The statute is summarized below.

> A person may petition the district court of the district where his or her criminal records are located to seal all of the records if he or she was never formally charged with the offense, the case was dismissed, or the individual was acquitted.

> The records will not be sealed if the individual was not charged or the case was dismissed due to a plea agreement in a separate case unless the petition is filed ten years after the date of

final disposition of all charges and he or she has not been charged with another criminal offense in that time.

Petitions must include the names of all agencies having the information that is the subject of the sealing order and information that identifies the records to be sealed.

The court will review the petition and decide whether to hold a hearing on the matter. If a hearing is granted, the individual requesting the sealing of records must notify the prosecuting attorney and the arresting agency by certified mail. The court finds that the harmful consequences to the individual outweigh the public interest in retaining the records, the court may order the records sealed.

There is an addition of an analogous section under 24-72-308.5 pertaining to sealing of criminal conviction records information for offenses involving controlled substances.

Effect of Expungement

If an individual successfully obtains an order sealing his or her records, he or she may state that no records exist. The records are not physically destroyed, however, and the court may permit inspection when requested by the individual or the prosecuting attorney.

Employers cannot require individuals to disclose any information contained in sealed records, and the individual may state on an application for employment that no such action ever occurred. The individual is required to disclose the information if applying with the Colorado Board of Law Examiners for admission to the State Bar.

Eligibility

Colorado permits the sealing of records for individuals who were never charged with the offense, the case was dismissed against them, or they were acquitted of all charges. Sealing of records is not permitted for offenses including: Class 1 or Class 2 misdemeanor traffic offenses, Class A or Class B traffic infractions, DUIs, or convictions involving unlawful sexual behavior. It should be noted that a DUI is defined in Colorado as driving under the influence of drugs or alcohol and requires a blood alcohol content of .08 or higher. It is a Class A traffic infraction for an individual under the age of 21 to drive with a blood alcohol content of at least .02 but not more than .05. If an individual under the age of 21 is charged with such an infraction, he or she may still be eligible for expungement according to Section 42-4-1715 of the Colorado Vehicles and Traffic Code.

Additionally, under 72-308.5 (4)(a) expungement will not be granted in cases where the conviction involved the sale, manufacture, or distribution of a controlled substance. Also, expungements will not be granted in:

1. Cases where the defendant has ever held a commercial driver's license; or
2. Cases where at the time of the offense the defendant was operating a commercial vehicle.

Expungement for Juveniles

Section 19-1-306 of the Colorado Children's Code entitled "Expungement for Juvenile Delinquent Records," allow for the sealing of records of juveniles. The statute closely parallels the statute pertaining to the sealing of records for adults, but it allows for relief from an actual conviction as well. The statute is summarized below.

An individual convicted of a criminal offense as a juvenile may petition the juvenile court for an order of expungement immediately upon a finding of not guilty, one year after the completion of a juvenile probation program, four years after release from custody or parole supervision, or ten years after release from custody or parole supervision if the individual is a repeat offender. No filing fee is required.

The court will conduct a hearing on the petition and may expunge all records if it finds:

1. The individual has not been convicted of a felony or misdemeanor since the original offense;

2. No felony, misdemeanor, or delinquency action is pending against the individual;

3. The court finds the individual sufficiently rehabilitated; and

4. Expungement is in the best interests of the individual and the community.

Juveniles convicted as aggravated or violent offenders and juveniles convicted of unlawful sexual behavior are not eligible for expungement.

Any record that is ordered expunged shall, notwithstanding any such order for expungement, be available to any judge and the probation department for use in any future juvenile or adult sentencing hearing regarding the person whose record was expunged.

Other Remedies

Article 4, Section 7 of the Colorado Constitution grants the Governor the power to grant full and unconditional pardons. Pardon applications are only accepted ten or more years after the completion of the sentence.

Contact Information:

(303) 866-2741

Clemency Director
Executive Chambers
136 State Capitol
Denver, CO 80203-1792

Conclusion

Although Colorado permits an individual to petition on their own behalf for the sealing of records without the assistance of an attorney, the ability to obtain an order granting such a petition depends entirely upon the judge and if, in his or her discretion, such an order is in the interest of justice. Legal arguments like these are best made by an experienced lawyer and the chances of obtaining an order sealing criminal records increases dramatically with a lawyer's assistance.

As we have said multiple times throughout this book "DO NOT TRY THIS AT HOME." There are tons of pitfalls and perils for those trying to obtain an expunction on their own without the help of an attorney. We've said it before and we'll say it now, ***do not try a "do it yourself expunction."***

The primary problem is "do it yourselfers" can stir up a long dormant and as of yet un-pursued case. In other words, if you go making haphazard inquiries in the wrong case you can arouse prosecutorial interest and fire up an investigation of you and your case/arrest. Thus, use the resource section of our website at www.ultimatesecondchance.com/resources to help find an attorney in your area.

CONNECTICUT

Introduction

In Connecticut, the Code of Criminal Procedure provides for the erasure of criminal records only where an individual is found not guilty or all charges against the individual are dismissed regardless of the reason for dismissal. In the event of a criminal conviction, the statutes provide for alternative relief in the form of a pardon.

The Law in Connecticut

Section 54-142a of Connecticut's Code of Criminal Procedure pertains to the erasure of criminal records. It outlines the circumstances in which an individual may petition to have his or her criminal record erased. The statute is summarized below.

> If an individual is found not guilty of a criminal charge or the charge is dismissed and the time to file an appeal has expired, all records relating to the charge are to be erased. Criminal records also are erased 13 months after the charge has been knolled by the superior court or the court of common pleas.

> Anyone convicted of crime who has received an absolute pardon for such offense may, at

any time after receiving the pardon, file a petition with the superior court for an order of erasure.

If an individual has been convicted of an offense that has been decriminalized after the date of the conviction, that individual may file a petition with the superior court for an order of erasure, and the superior court shall order that records pertaining to such case be physically destroyed.

Section 54-56e of the Connecticut Code of Criminal Procedure, entitled "Accelerated Pretrial Rehabilitation," establishes a probation program available to a certain class of non-violent offenders. The statute provides that if an individual successfully completes the program, he or she may petition to have the criminal charges dismissed and the record erased. The statute is summarized below.

The court may decide to place an individual in a pretrial rehabilitation program. The program is not available to individuals charged with Class A or B felonies, driving under the influence, sexual assault, vehicular manslaughter or assault, or the possession of child pornography. After successfully completing the program, the individual can petition the court to have the charges dismissed, and upon dismissal, all the records are to be erased.

Eligibility

The Connecticut statutes grant the option of erasure only when an individual is found not guilty or if the charge has been dismissed. Individuals may be eligible for erasure if the charges were dismissed due to successful completion of the accelerated pretrial rehabilitation program. In other words, the individual does not need to prove to the court he or she is factually innocent in order to receive erasure as is the case in several other states. Erasure applies to all criminal offenses, regardless of type. Erasure is not available, however, for an individual found not guilty by reason of mental disease.

Effect of Erasure

If an individual successfully obtains an order for erasure, the agency in charge of the records must safeguard the records against unauthorized access or dissemination. If three years have passed since the final disposition of an offense, the individual may request that the criminal records be physically destroyed. The individual is considered as never having been arrested and may swear under oath to that effect.

Erasure for Juveniles

Like many other states, Connecticut grants erasure more readily for juvenile offenders. Section 54-760 of the Connecticut Code of Criminal Procedure applies specifically to youthful offenders and sets forth the requirements for erasure of juvenile records. The statute is summarized below.

> Whenever a youthful offender is discharged from court supervision or custody, all records automatically are erased if the juvenile reaches 21 years of age without receiving a felony conviction. The individual is considered as never having been arrested.

Other Remedies

Section §54-142l of the Connecticut Code of Criminal Procedure, in addition to establishing the availability of erasure, outlines the steps an individual may take to ensure his or her criminal record is accurate. The statute is summarized below.

> An individual can challenge the completeness and accuracy of his or her criminal record by sending written notice of the challenge to the Bureau of Identification. The notice must contain a sworn statement that the challenge is made in good faith and all the information contained in the challenge is accurate. The Bureau of Identification will conduct an audit of the record and send the results to the individual who challenged the record within 60 days. The individual may appeal an adverse decision of the Bureau.

In the event of a criminal conviction, there are

alternative methods available for relief. Five years after the successful completion of a sentence and probation put in place due to a criminal conviction, the individual subject to the conviction may apply for a pardon with the Connecticut Board of Pardons and Paroles. If successful in obtaining a pardon, the individual becomes eligible for erasure.

Connecticut Board of Pardon and Parole contact information:
(203) 805-6607
Pardon Board Coordinator
55 West Main Street, Suite 520
Waterbury, CT 06702

Conclusion

As we have said multiple times throughout this book "DO NOT TRY THIS AT HOME." There are tons of pitfalls and perils for those trying to obtain erasure on their own without the help of an attorney. We've said it before and we'll say it now, *do not try a do it yourself expunction.*

The primary problem is "do it yourselfers" can stir up a long dormant and as of yet un-pursued case. In other words, if you go making haphazard inquiries in the wrong case you can arouse prosecutorial interest and fire up an investigation of you and your case/arrest. Thus, use the resource section of our website at www.ultimatesecondchance.com/resources to help find an attorney in your area.

DELAWARE

Introduction

In Delaware the law governing expungement is very clear. The statutes set forth the exact requirements for obtaining expungement, and the purpose of expungement law. There are also numerous programs implemented by the state that give first-time offenders the opportunity to clear their criminal records.

The Law in Delaware

Sections 4371 through 4375 of the Delaware Code of Crimes and Criminal Procedure outline the purpose of expungement, the effect an expungement has on one's criminal record, as well as the procedure for obtaining expungement. The statutes are summarized below.

If a person is charged with a criminal offense and he or she is acquitted or the charge is dismissed, he or she may petition the Superior Court to expunge the records relating to the charge. A copy of the petition must be sent to the Attorney General, and the attorney general may file an objection within 30 days.

Unless the Court believes a hearing is necessary, it will make determinations without a hearing. If the Court finds that the existence of the record creates circumstances that constitute a manifest injustice to the individual, the court will enter an order expunging the records.

The existence of a previous conviction on the individual's record will prevent the court from granting an order for expungement.

In Delaware, the statutes establish several programs available for first-time offenders and individuals convicted of misdemeanor offenses that allow them to clear their criminal records. Section 4218 of the Delaware Crimes and Criminal Procedure Code, entitled "Probation Before Judgment," outlines one such program. Upon an individual's successful completion of a probationary period and the fulfillment of certain conditions, the court will discharge an individual without judgment. Those individuals discharged after completing the program are eligible for expungement.

Eligibility

The purpose of expungement law in Delaware is to protect innocent people from the negative effects of a criminal record. To be eligible for expunction, a person either must be acquitted or have his or her charges dismissed. This is true for any type of crime. The individual does not need to be factually innocent to be eligible for expungement. Charges may be dismissed for any reason including discharge from probation before judgment.

Effect of Expungement

If the court grants an order for expungement, all the records are removed from the files, and placed in a separate location. The information contained in the records is not to be released for any reason unless by court order. The individual does not have to disclose information of the arrest for any reason.

Juvenile Expungement

Like many states, juvenile offenders in Delaware find it easier to obtain an expungement order. Section 1001 of the Delaware Code of Court and Judicial Procedures outlines expungement law regarding juvenile offenders. The statute is summarized below.

An individual charged with a criminal offense under the age of 18 may petition the court to expunge all records of the offense, if:

1. He or she was acquitted;

2. The charges were dismissed; or

3. He or she was convicted and three years have passed since the original conviction without another conviction.

The court may grant a hearing, and if there is no opposition to the expungement, the court will order that all information concerning the arrest be destroyed.

Expungement is not available to juveniles convicted of the following crimes: second degree murder, first degree arson, and first degree burglary.

If a juvenile receives a pardon from the Governor, his or her criminal record automatically is expunged.

Other Remedies

Article VII of the Delaware Constitution gives the Governor the power to grant an unconditional pardon. A pardon effectually restores all civil rights that were lost as the result of a criminal conviction. A pardon is not an expungement and a criminal record will still exist. Applications for pardon are made in writing through the Secretary of State.

For more information contact:

Secretary of State's Office
401 Federal Street, Suite 3,
Dover, DE 19901

Conclusion

Although the Delaware statutes provide that an individual may petition the court for expungement on his or her own behalf, it is a complicated process. Obtaining a pardon in the State of Delaware is equally complicated and requires notifying several state officials and gathering massive quantities of information. Anyone looking to clear his or her record stands a better chance with the help of an experienced attorney.

As we have said multiple times throughout this book "DO NOT TRY THIS AT HOME." There are tons of pitfalls and perils for those trying to obtain an expunction on their own without the help of an attorney. We've said it before and we'll say it now, ***do not try a do it yourself expunction***.

The primary problem is "do it yourselfers" can stir up a long dormant and as of yet un-pursued case. In other words, if you go making haphazard inquiries in the wrong case you can arouse prosecutorial interest and fire up an investigation of you and your case/arrest. Thus, use the resource section of our website at www.ultimatesecondchance.com/resources to help find an attorney in your area.

FLORIDA

Introduction

In Florida, the statutes regarding expunction clearly outline the requirements that must be met in order to obtain relief from a criminal record. The requirements, however, are extremely rigid, and in the end, it is the judge's decision alone that determines whether an expunction order is granted.

The Law in Florida

Section 943.0585 of Florida's Code of Criminal Procedures and Corrections, entitled "Court Ordered Expunction of Criminal History Records," sets out the procedure for obtaining an expunction. The statute is relatively straightforward and the Florida Rules of Criminal Procedure even provide copies of the forms that applicants should use. The statute is summarized below.

Before petitioning the court for expunction, an individual must apply to the Department of Law Enforcement for a Certificate of Eligibility for Expunction. To obtain that certificate, the individual must pay a $75 processing fee, submit a certified copy of the disposition of the charge to which the petition for expunction relates, and submit a written, certified statement from the state attorney or statewide prosecutor indicating:

1. That an indictment was not filed in the case, or;

2. That the indictment was dismissed; and

3. That the offense is one that may be expunged.

The Department will issue the Certificate of Eligibility if the individual:

1. Has never been convicted of a criminal offense before;

2. Was not convicted of the charge to which the petition relates;

3. Has never received an expunction before;

4. Is no longer under court supervision;

5. Does not have to wait ten years before becoming eligible for an expunction because the charges were dismissed prior to trial or during trial; and

6. Was charged with the type of crime that may be expunged.

After receiving a Certificate of Eligibility, an individual must file it along with the petition to the court requesting expunction. The petition must identify the grounds on which it is based and the records to be expunged. The petition must include an affidavit that identifies the statutory grounds for expunction and the facts that support the petition. The petition form and affidavit are found in Rule 3.989 of the Florida Rules of Criminal Procedure.

A copy of the petition also must be sent to the state attorney or the statewide prosecutor who may respond to the court regarding the completed petition. The courts in Florida have jurisdiction over the maintenance, expunction, and correction of criminal records. Any court, in its discretion, can order expungement of an individual's entire criminal record or any portion thereof, based on the petition.

Eligibility

In Florida, an individual is eligible for expunction if he or she was never adjudicated guilty, or convicted of the offense for which he or she was charged. An individual need not be factually innocent to be is eligible for expunction. If a sentence was withheld in exchange for probation, an individual becomes eligible for expunction upon the successful completion of probation. The statutes, however, contain a laundry list of offenses which may not be expunged if the individual pled guilty or *nolo contendere*, regardless of whether adjudication was withheld. Those offenses that may not be expunged include: sexual misconduct, kidnapping, sexual battery, computer pornography, communications fraud, any crime committed while in public office, selling or buying of minors, drug trafficking, or any type of dangerous crime.

Effect of Expunction

Any criminal record ordered expunged must be physically destroyed by the arresting agency, and court, however, a copy is retained by the Department of Law Enforcement. That copy is to be kept confidential and is not available to any person without a court order. The individual who is the subject of an expunged record can deny the arrests, except when he or she:

1. Is applying for employment with a criminal justice agency;

2. Is a defendant in a criminal prosecution;

3. Applies for a later expunction;

4. Is seeking admission to the Florida Bar;

5. Is seeking employment with the Department of Children and Family Services or the Department of Juvenile Justice; or

6. Is seeking employment with the Department of Education.

Expunction for Juveniles

Section 943.0515 of the Florida Code of Criminal Procedure and Corrections, entitled "Retention of Criminal History Records of Minors," establishes the requirements for obtaining an expunction of records relating to an offense committed as a juvenile. The statute is summarized below.

The Criminal Justice Information Program must keep records of serious or habitual juvenile offenders or juveniles committed to a juvenile correctional facility or juvenile prison for five years after the date they turn 21 years old. The records may be expunged at that time. If the minor does not fall into the category of serious or habitual offender, the records may be expunged five years after his or her 19th birthday. If the minor is convicted as an adult of a forcible felony, the record must become part of his or her adult record.

Section 943.0582 of the Florida Code of Criminal Procedure and Corrections makes expunction available to minors who successfully complete a pre-arrest, post-arrest, or teen court diversionary program. This type of program is strictly limited to minors arrested for non-violent misdemeanors. The statute is summarized below.

The Department of Law Enforcement can expunge the non-judicial criminal record of a minor who successfully completes a pre-arrest or post-arrest diversion program if:

1. The minor submits an application expunction no later than six months after completing the program;

2. The minor submits an official written statement from the state attorney certifying the successful completion of the program;

3. The program expressly permits expunction;

4. The arrest was made for a non-violent misdemeanor; and

5. The minor has not been charged with a criminal offense before.

An individual who receives an expunction due to the completion of a diversionary program as a minor is not prevented from seeking an expunction from a later charge as an adult.

Other Remedies

Article IV, Section 8(a) of the Florida Constitution grants the Governor the power of executive clemency. An individual convicted of a criminal offense in Florida may apply with the Office of Executive Clemency for relief ranging from a restoration of civil rights to a full unconditional pardon. The Board will not consider an application for a full pardon unless ten years have passed since the completion of probation or parole. Neither a full pardon, nor any other type of clemency, will expunge a criminal record.

Office of Executive Clemency contact information:

(850) 488-2952
Coordinator, Office of Executive Clemency
2601 Blair Stone Road
Building C, Room 244
Tallahassee, FL 32399-2450

Conclusion

Florida provides that anyone may apply for an expunction on his or her own behalf. It is the judge's decision alone that determines whether an expunction will be granted in any particular case. Your chances of convincing the judge that an order granting expunction is the proper course of action greatly improve with the help of an experienced attorney.

As we have said multiple times throughout this book "DO NOT TRY THIS AT HOME." There are tons of pitfalls and perils for those trying to obtain an expunction on their own without the help of an attorney. We've said it before and we'll say it now, *do not try a do it yourself expunction.*

The primary problem is "do it yourselfers" can stir up a long dormant and as of yet un-pursued case. In other words, if you go making haphazard inquiries in the wrong case you can arouse prosecutorial interest and fire up an investigation of you and your case/arrest. Thus, use the resource section of our website at www.ultimatesecondchance.com/resources to help find an attorney in your area.

GEORGIA

Introduction

In Georgia, the statutes providing for the expungement of criminal records are subject to varying interpretations. The guidelines set forth in the statutory language are not clear, and due to the ambiguity, different individuals may receive varying results, depending on the individual facts of the case and the judge who makes the final decision.

The Law in Georgia

Section 35-3-37 of the Georgia Law Enforcement Officers and Agencies Code, entitled "Inspection of Records; Correction," establishes the procedure an individual must follow in order to inspect his or her criminal record. The statute also outlines the procedures and requirements an individual must satisfy in order to obtain the relief of correction or possible expungement of his or her criminal record. The statute is summarized below.

An individual may make a written request to the Georgia Crime Information Center to inspect his or her criminal records. If the individual feels the records are inaccurate or incomplete, he or she can request the agency in charge of the records to expunge, modify, or supplement them. The individual may appeal the agency's decision not to act to the superior court within 30 days. The court will conduct a hearing on the matter, and if the court finds the record is inaccurate, incomplete, or misleading, the court can order the record expunged, modified, or supplemented by an explanatory notation. The statute reserves expungement, however, for exceptional cases in which the court finds the interest of the individual in having the records expunged outweighs the interest of the State in keeping the records.

If an individual was arrested for a criminal offense and later released without being charged or if the charges were dismissed, the individual can make request in writing to the agency in charge of the records to have them expunged. The agency will forward the request to the prosecuting attorney for review.

An individual has the right to have his or her record of the arrest expunged if the prosecuting attorney determines:

1. The charge was dismissed;

2. No other criminal charges are pending against the individual; and

3. The individual has not been convicted

of a similar offense in the past five years.

If the agency refuses to expunge the records, the individual may file an action in the superior court where the agency is located. The decision will be upheld only if it is determined that the individual did not meet the above criteria.

Eligibility

In Georgia, an individual may request that his or her criminal records be expunged in the event he or she was never charged of an offense or if the charges were dismissed. If charges are filed and later dismissed, however, the record will not be expunged, if the dismissal was the result of:

1. A plea agreement;

2. The court barring the government from introducing material evidence;

3. The refusal of a material witness to testify or the unavailability of a witness.

In addition, expungement will be denied where:

1. The individual was arrested on other criminal charges and the prosecuting attorney chose not to prosecute for

reasons of judicial economy;

2. The individual successfully completed a pretrial diversion program that does not provide for expungement;

3. The conduct which resulted in the arrest of the individual was part of a pattern of criminal activity; or

4. The individual had diplomatic immunity.

Effect of Expungement

When a court orders that a record be expunged, the agency in control of the record must destroy it. Any part of the record that cannot physically be destroyed, or that the prosecuting attorney determines must be preserved, must be restricted by the agency and cannot be disclosed to anyone unless by court order. Restricted records may be made available to criminal justice officials upon written application for official investigative purposes.

Expungement for Juveniles

In Georgia, there is no separate statutory authority regarding the expungement of criminal records of juvenile offenders. Section 15-11-45 of the Georgia Code of Juvenile Proceedings, however, outlines the circumstances in which a juvenile may be arrested. The Code uses the term "taking into custody" instead of "arrest" to serve protective functions for juvenile offenders. It allows a juvenile to answer negatively to questions on employment, educational, financial, or other applications seeking information regarding arrests, and it limits access to police records involving juveniles.

Other Remedies

Article IV, section II, paragraph II of the Georgia Constitution establishes the Georgia Board of Pardons and Paroles. An individual convicted of a criminal offense in the State may apply for a pardon that Board. The Board considers only those applications submitted five years or more after the individual has completed the sentence stemming from his or her criminal conviction. No pardon is automatic and the Board judges the merits of each individual case.

Georgia State Board of Pardons and Paroles contact information:

(404) 656-5651
State Board of Pardons and Paroles
2 Martin Luther King, Jr. Dr. SE
Suite 458, Balcony Level,
East Tower
Atlanta, GA 30334-4909

Conclusion

The Georgia statutes regarding expungement of a criminal record are subject to interpretation. The language is unclear and the ability to obtain expungement may depend solely on which judge hears the case. A judge will grant an expungement if it is in the interest of justice. An individual stands a better chance of successfully convincing a judge expungement is the appropriate remedy with the help of an experienced attorney.

As we have said multiple times throughout this book "DO NOT TRY THIS AT HOME." There are tons of pitfalls and perils for those trying to obtain an expunction on their own without the help of an attorney. We've said it before and we'll say it now, ***do not try a do it yourself expunction.***

The primary problem is "do it yourselfers" can stir up a long dormant and as of yet un-pursued case. In other words, if you go making haphazard inquiries in the wrong case you can arouse prosecutorial interest and fire up an investigation of you and your case/arrest. Thus, use the resource section of our website at www.ultimatesecondchance.com/resources to help find an attorney in your area.

GUAM

Introduction

Guam statutes provide relatively straightforward, almost simplistic, definitions and requirements for expungement. Expungement is only available to a limited class of individuals and criminal records, although sealed, are never really destroyed. Assuming an individual is eligible for expungement, relief is granted upon request.

The Law in Guam

Section 11.10 of the Guam Code of Criminal Procedure, entitled "Expungement of Records," explains when an order of expungement may be obtained. An individual must petition the court for expungement, but the right to obtain one is automatic and is not subject to the discretion of the judge, as in several other territories. The statute is summarized below:

An individual's criminal record is expunged when:

1. The individual is acquitted of the charge;

2. The prosecuting attorney decides not to prosecute; or

3. The statute of limitations in which to file charges has passed without such charges being filed.

For individuals with criminal convictions involving drugs, Section 67.412 of the Guam Code of Crimes and Corrections provides some relief in the form of probation with a deferred judgment, also called a conditional discharge. If an individual successfully completes the probationary period, he or she is discharged and his or her records are eligible for expungement. The statute is summarized below.

If an individual who never has been convicted of a drug-related offense before is found guilty of possession of a controlled substance, the court may defer judgment and place the individual on probation. After successful completion of the terms and conditions of the probation, the court will discharge the individual and dismiss the charges against him or her. Discharge and dismissal are not a conviction, and an individual may only take advantage of it once.

After discharge and dismissal, the individual can apply to the court for an order to expunge all records relating to the offense. After a hearing on the matter, if the court finds that the individual was dismissed and discharged, it will enter the order.

Eligibility

As outlined above, the relief of expungement in Guam is reserved for a limited class of individuals: those who were acquitted, those against whom no charges were brought, and those with drug possession charges who successfully completed a conditional discharge probationary program.

Effect of Expungement

In Guam, the term "expungement" means the sealing of records to everyone outside of the law enforcement agencies and other federal agencies. An individual whose records have been ordered expunged is restored to the status he or she occupied before the arrest or charge, and the individual is never required to acknowledge the arrest or charge in response to any questions for any purpose.

Juvenile Expungement

Title 9, Chapter 83, of the Guam Code, entitled "The Youth Correction Act," establishes punishment alternatives and options for youth offenders. The Director of the Board of Parole may place an individual on probation or sentence him or her to supervision. When the juvenile unconditionally is discharged by the Board, the conviction automatically is set aside and the Board will issue to the youth offender a certificate to that effect.

Other Remedies

The Department of Corrections, Parole Services Division investigates pardon applications and forwards them to the Pardon Review Board. The Pardon Review Board then evaluates the applications and makes recommendations to the Governor. A full pardon restores the rights an individual lost due to a criminal conviction.

The Department of Corrections, Parole Service Division contact information:
> (671) 473-7001
> Parole Services Division
> Suite 507 Pacific News Building
> Hagatna, GU

Conclusion

As we have said multiple times throughout this book "DO NOT TRY THIS AT HOME." There are tons of pitfalls and perils for those trying to obtain an expunction on their own without the help of an attorney. We've said it before and we'll say it now, *do not try a do it yourself expunction.*

The primary problem is "do it yourselfers" can stir up a long dormant and as of yet un-pursued case. In other words, if you go making haphazard inquiries in the wrong case you can arouse prosecutorial interest and fire up an investigation of you and your case/arrest. Thus, use the resource section of our website at www.ultimatesecondchance.com/resources to help find an attorney in your area.

HAWAII

Introduction

In Hawaii, the statutes set forth the general eligibility requirements for obtaining an expungement of criminal records. The statutes also establish several alternative sentencing programs for first-time, non-violent offenders that allow for the relief of expungement in a greater array of circumstances.

The Law in Hawaii

Section 831-3.2 of the Hawaii Crimes and Criminal Proceedings Statutes, entitled "Expungement Orders," creates the relief of expungement and establishes the eligibility requirements. The statute is summarized below.

> An individual arrested or charged with a criminal offense, but never convicted, may apply to the attorney general in writing for an expungement order. The attorney general will issue the order in most circumstances, but expungement will not be granted:
>
> 1. If a conviction was not obtained due to bail forfeiture;
>
> 2. For five years after an arrest for a petty

misdemeanor where conviction was not obtained due to bail forfeiture;

3. If a conviction was not obtained because the individual fled the jurisdiction;

4. If an individual was acquitted due to mental or physical defect; or

5. Until one year has passed from the discharge of an individual in the case of a deferred acceptance of guilty plea or *nolo contendere* plea.

If the individual is eligible for expungement, the attorney general will issue a certificate stating that the expungement order has been issued.

Section 853-1 of the Hawaii Crimes and Criminal Proceedings Statutes establishes a probationary program for certain individuals who wish to plead guilty in exchange for a deferred adjudication. Upon successful completion of the program, the individual may have the records relating to the offense expunged. The statute is summarized below.

If a defendant voluntarily pleads guilty or *nolo contendere* to a felony or misdemeanor before the trial, and the court feels that the individual is not likely to repeat the offense and that the ends of justice do not require the full penalties, the court, without accepting the plea, may defer further proceedings.

When the individual completes the probationary period and fulfills all the terms and conditions, the court will discharge him or her and dismiss the charges. Discharge and dismissal is not a conviction, and the individual may apply for expungement one year after his or her discharge.

Section 706-622.5 of the Hawaii Crimes and Criminal Proceedings Statutes establishes a probationary substance abuse program for first-time drug offenders. Once an individual has completed the program, he or she may have the record of the conviction expunged. The statute is summarized below.

An individual convicted for the first time of any offense involving the possession or use of drugs or drug paraphernalia is eligible for probation if:

1. The court has determined that the individual is nonviolent;

2. A counselor has evaluated the individual and determined he or she is in need of drug treatment for dependency or abuse; and

3. The individual is ordered to supervised treatment and in fact obtains treatment

from a private program in accordance with the treatment plan determined by a drug counselor.

After successfully completing the substance abuse program and probation, the individual may petition the court in writing to expunge the record of the conviction. The court will issue a court order to expunge the record, but the individual is eligible only once as a first-time offender.

Another available means of expungement is Section 712-1256 of the Hawaii Penal Code, entitled "Expunging of Court Records." This relief is available only to individuals who were under the age of 20 at the time of the offense. The statute is summarized below.

When an individual finally is dismissed from an order of conditional discharge, (which is similar to probation) the individual may apply to the court to expunge all of his or her records if he or she was under the age of 20 at the time of the offense. The court will conduct a hearing to determine if the individual meets all the above conditions, and if so, the court will enter an order of expungement.

Eligibility

In Hawaii, there are several options which allow the relief of expungement. Generally, the court will expunge any offense if there was never a conviction because, for example, the charges were dismissed, or the individual was acquitted. First-time drug offenders, individuals who enter a deferred acceptance of guilty plea, and individuals under 20 years of age at the time of the offense may be required to complete special programs that do not result in convictions. The individuals are eligible for expungement as well.

Effect of Expungement

In Hawaii, when the court enters an order for expungement, all the records subject to the order are forwarded to the attorney general for placement in a confidential file. Records may not be released except upon inquiry by:

1. A court or agency investigating for the court;

2. An government agency for employment purposes; or

3. A law enforcement agency in the course of its duties.

Upon entry of the expungement order, the individual is treated as never having been arrested, and is never required to acknowledge the arrest or charge in response to any question for any purpose.

Juvenile Expungement

Section 571-88 of the Hawaii Family Code, entitled

"Orders Expunging Juvenile Arrest Records," sets out the requirements that must be fulfilled in order to request a court order expungement of juvenile arrest records. The statute is summarized below.

> An individual may apply to the court in writing for an order expunging his or her juvenile arrest record if the record meets the following criteria:
>
> 1. The information was never given to the prosecuting attorney or court and
>
>   a. The individual was not counseled and released by the police; or
>
>   b. The individual was counseled and released by the police and the person has become an adult; or
>
> 2. The information was given to the prosecuting attorney or court and
>
>   a. The individual was not convicted; or
>
>   b. The matter was dismissed with prejudice.
>
> If the individual is eligible for expungement, the court will give him or her a certificate stating that the expungement order has been issued.

Other Remedies

Article IV, Section V of the Hawaiian Constitution grants the Governor the power to issue pardons to individuals. The Director of Public Safety and the Paroling Authority initially evaluate pardon applications then refer them to the Governor for consideration. Pardon applications are provided by the Hawaii Paroling Authority.

Hawaii Paroling Authority Contact Information:

(808) 587-1295
Hawaii Paroling Authority
ATTENTION:
Paroles and Pardons Administrator
1177 Alakea Street, Ground Floor
Honolulu, HI 96813

Conclusion

In Hawaii, the statutes provide for several different opportunities to obtain an expungement of criminal records. All requirements are strictly enforced, and many find the process extremely complicated. The chances of successfully obtaining expungement increase dramatically with the help of an experienced attorney.

As we have said multiple times throughout this book "DO NOT TRY THIS AT HOME." There are tons of pitfalls and perils for those trying to obtain an expunction on their own without the help of an attorney. We've said it before and we'll say it now, ***do not try a do it yourself expunction.***

The primary problem is "do it yourselfers" can stir up a long dormant and as of yet un-pursued case. In other words, if you go making haphazard inquiries in the wrong case you can arouse prosecutorial interest and fire up an investigation of you and your case/arrest. Thus, use the resource section of our website at www.ultimatesecondchance.com/resources to help find an attorney in your area.

IDAHO

Introduction

In Idaho, statutes regarding expungement are considerably vague. The statutes do not detail procedures to follow when attempting to obtain a grant of expungement, and they do not lay out the effect expungement has on a criminal record. Nevertheless, the state provides opportunities for expungement in a variety of circumstances.

The Law in Idaho

Section 67-3004, Chapter 30 of the Idaho Code of State Government and State Affairs, entitled "Fingerprinting and Identification," outlines the police department's duties with respect to criminal record information. The section also contains a vague reference to the relief of expungement of criminal records, but the statute does not outline a procedure for requesting expungement or the effect of expungement. The pertinent parts of the statute are summarized below.

> The Idaho State Police Department Bureau of Criminal Identification collects and files fingerprints and identifying data on individuals who have been arrested in the state.

If an individual was arrested but not charged of the offense within one year of the arrest, or the individual was acquitted, he or she may make a written request to the Idaho State Police Department to have the fingerprint and criminal history record expunged.

Section 19-2604 of the Idaho Code of Criminal Procedure, entitled "Discharge of Defendant — Amendment of Judgment," outlines the availability of expungement or the reduction of the sentence after the successful completion of a probationary period. If an individual is granted a suspended sentence and placed on probation, the individual becomes eligible for expungement if the charge is dismissed after satisfactorily completing the probation. Individuals whose charges are reduced are not eligible for expungement. The statute is summarized below.

If an individual was convicted of a criminal offense, but the sentence was suspended or withheld subject to the successful completion of a probationary program, the individual may apply to have his or her sentence set aside upon completion of probation. If the court is convinced that it is in the public interest, the court may terminate the sentence or set aside the conviction and dismiss the case and discharge the individual.

If the court suspended the sentence during the first 180 days and the court placed individual on probation, the court may amend the judgment of conviction to "confinement in a penal facility" for the number of days served prior to suspension, and may reduce the conviction to a misdemeanor conviction.

Convictions for sexual abuse or exploitation of a child will not be reduced to misdemeanors or expunged from a person's criminal record.

Eligibility

Idaho's statutes regarding expungement are vague. The above statutes seem to dictate that to be eligible for the relief of expungement, an individual must either be acquitted of the offense for which he or she was arrested, never charged for the offense for which he or she was arrested, or have all charges stemming from the arrest dropped. If the court discharges an individual and dismisses the charges against him or her after the completion of probation, the individual may be eligible to have the record of the offense expunged.

Effect of Expungement

Idaho statutes do not outline the effect of expungement or state whether the records are destroyed or sequestered and in what circumstances they may be released.

Expungement for Juveniles

Idaho, like many other states, the relief of expungement is more widely available to juvenile offenders. Section 20-525A of the Idaho Code outlines the availability of expungement for juveniles. The statute is much clearer than the Idaho statutes concerning adult expungement and even detail the effect of expungement on a juvenile record. The statute is summarized below.

> Any juvenile convicted of a felony offense or committed to the Department of Juvenile Corrections can petition the court for expungement of his or her records after five years have passed since his or her release from custody or supervision or upon turning 18 years of age, whichever occurs last.

> Any juvenile convicted of a misdemeanor can petition the court for expungement of his or her records after one year has passed since his or her release from supervision or upon turning 18 years of age, whichever occurs later.

> The court will hold a hearing, and if it determines it is in the interests of justice, the court shall order all records relating to the offense sealed. The case shall be considered never to have occurred and the juvenile may state he or she has never been arrested when questioned. Inspection of sealed records may be permitted only by court order.

> The court may not expunge convictions for violent crimes, or manufacturing and trafficking drugs.

Other Remedies

In Idaho, like many other states, sexual offenders

must register with a centralized state agency. Section 18-8310, Chapter 83 of the Idaho Code of Crimes and Punishments, entitled "Release from Registration Requirements — Expungement," establishes the opportunity for a convicted sex offender to expunge his or her records from the sex offender registry. This statute applies only to the sex offender registry and does not state how expungement of records from the registry affects criminal records as a whole. The statute is summarized below.

> An individual other than a repeat offender, an individual convicted of an aggravated offense, or a violent sexual predator, may, after ten years from the date the individual was released from custody or probation, petition the district court for hearing to determine whether the individual may be exempted from registering as a sexual offender. In the petition the petitioner shall:
>
> 1. Provide evidence that the individual is not a risk to commit a new violation;
>
> 2. Provide an affidavit indicating he or she has no criminal charge pending;
>
> 3. Provide proof of service of the petition on the county prosecuting attorney; and
>
> 4. Provide a copy of the conviction for which the individual had to report as a sexual offender.

The court may grant a hearing if the petition is sufficient, and the court may exempt the individual from reporting if it finds the individual is not likely to commit another offense. The court may order the information regarding the individual expunged from the central registry.

Article IV, Section 7 of the Idaho Constitution establishes the Idaho Board of Pardons and grants the Board and the Governor the power to grant unconditional pardons for criminal offenses. The Board and the Governor will not consider applications for pardons for non-violent and non-sexual offenses until at least three years have elapsed since the completion of punishment. The Board and the Governor will not consider applications for pardons for violent and sexual offenses until at least five years have elapsed since the completion of punishment. Applications for pardon may be obtained from the Idaho Commission of Pardons and Parole.

Commission of Pardons and Parole contact information:

(208) 334-2520
Commission of Pardons and Parole
P.O. Box 83720
Statehouse Mail
Boise, ID 83720

Conclusion

Applying for expungement in the State of Idaho can be an extremely confusing process due to the unclear statutes. In order to obtain an order of expungement in certain circumstances, you must argue the merits of the case and convince the judge expungement is the proper remedy. Your chances of success improve tremendously with the help of an experienced lawyer.

As we have said multiple times throughout this book "DO NOT TRY THIS AT HOME." There are tons of pitfalls and perils for those trying to obtain an expunction on their own without the help of an attorney. We've said it before and we'll say it now, *do not try a do it yourself expunction.*

The primary problem is "do it yourselfers" can stir up a long dormant and as of yet un-pursued case. In other words, if you go making haphazard inquiries in the wrong case you can arouse prosecutorial interest and fire up an investigation of you and your case/arrest. Thus, use the resource section of our website at www.ultimatesecondchance.com/resources to help find an attorney in your area.

ILLINOIS

Introduction

In Illinois, the law regarding expungement is very detailed and complex. Many circumstances may make an individual eligible for the relief of expungement. The procedures for obtaining expungement and eligibility requirements therefore are spelled out in the Illinois Criminal Identification Act.

The Law in Illinois

Section 5 of The Illinois Criminal Identification Act, entitled "Arrest Records: Expungement," outlines the availability and procedure for obtaining expungement of criminal records. Expungement means the sealing of criminal records, and a wide variety of offenders may be eligible for relief. The Act is summarized below.

> If an individual has no previous convictions and is acquitted or released without being convicted, he or she may petition for expungement. Several other circumstances may make an individual eligible for expungement.

A court may seal records when an individual was:

1. Acquitted without being convicted;

2. Convicted but the conviction was reversed;

3. Placed on misdemeanor supervision for an offense, at least three years have passed since the completion of the supervision, and the individual has not received another conviction in that time; or

4. Convicted and at least four years have passed since the last conviction or term of any sentence or probation, and the individual has not received another conviction in that time.

An individual seeking this relief must file a petition with the clerk of the court where the charges were brought. The petition must contain the individual's name, date of birth, current address, each charge, each case number, the date of each charge, the identity of the arresting authority, and any other information the court may require. Individuals eligible for expungement due to the successful completion of a drug offender probation program also must include drug testing information.

When the clerk receives the petition for expungement, he or she will notify the State's Attorney or prosecutor, the Department of State Police, and the arresting agency. If they fail to object to the petition within 30 days, the court will enter an order granting or denying the petition without a hearing. If an objection is timely filed, the court will hold a hearing to determine whether to issue the order. The decision to grant an order of expungement is within the court's discretion.

Eligibility

As the Act states, individuals acquitted or released without being convicted are eligible for expungement if they have no previous convictions. However, individuals who were convicted also may be eligible to have their records sealed. For example, certain individuals placed on probation may petition for expungement two to five years after discharge and dismissal of supervision. All municipal ordinance violations and misdemeanors may be sealed, with the exception of DUIs, sexual offenses, violations of orders of protection, crimes of violence, and Class A misdemeanor violations of the Humane Care for Animals Act. Records of misdemeanors and Class 4 felonies involving prostitution and first-time drug offenses may be sealed. Individuals who have been convicted and receive a pardon from the Governor specifically authorizing expungement are eligible for relief.

Effect of Expungement

When the judge enters an order for expungement, the information is to be erased from the records of the arresting authority and impounded by the court after five years. The Department of State Police must seal the records which may be released only to the arresting authority, the State's Attorney, the Department of Corrections and the court in the event of a later arrest.

Expungement for Juveniles

Section 5-915 of the Illinois Juvenile Court Act, entitled "Expungement of Juvenile Law Enforcement and Court Records," provides detailed steps and forms to be used by individuals requesting expungement of juvenile arrest records. The statute is summarized below.

When a juvenile reaches age 17 or when all juvenile court proceedings relating to him or her have ended, he or she may petition the court to expunge records relating to incidents that took place before his or her 17th birthday, if the juvenile was:

1. Arrested but charges were filed;

2. Charged but found not guilty;

3. Placed under supervision and the order has since terminated; or

4. Adjudicated for an offense which would be a Class B misdemeanor, Class C misdemeanor, or petty offense if committed by an adult.

An individual may petition the court to expunge all records relating to incidents that took place before his or her 17th birthday, except those based upon first degree murder and sex offenses, if he or she has had no convictions since his or her 17th birthday, and he or she has reached the age of 21 or five years have elapsed since the termination of all juvenile proceedings against him or her, whichever is later.

An individual seeking this relief must file a petition with the clerk of the court where the charges were brought. The petition form is found in Section 5-915 of the Illinois Juvenile Court Act. Upon receipt of the petition for expungement, the clerk will notify the State's Attorney or prosecutor, the Department of State Police, and the arresting agency. If they fail to object to the petition within 30 days, the court will enter an order granting or denying the petition without a hearing. If an objection is timely filed, the court will hold a hearing to determine whether to issue the order.

Once a case is expunged, it is treated as if it never occurred and the juvenile may not be required to disclose that he or she had a juvenile record. With the exception of law enforcement agencies, an expunged juvenile record may not be considered in employment matters, certification, licensing, revocation of certification or licensure, or registration.

Other Remedies

In Illinois, the Governor may use the power of Executive Clemency to pardon criminal offenders. Individuals who receive full pardons from the Governor are eligible to apply for expungement. Pardon applications are addressed to the Governor but actually sent to and evaluated by the Illinois Prisoner Review Board. Copies of the pardon application must also be sent to the sentencing judge and the state attorney for the county in which the conviction took place.

Prisoner Review Board contact information:

(217) 782-7273
Illinois Prisoner Review Board
319 East Madison,
Suite A
Springfield, IL 62701

Conclusion

In Illinois, the statutes governing expungement are extremely detailed and complex. In the end, the decision to grant an expungement is within the judge's discretion. To be successful, you must be convincing. The chances of obtaining an expungement increase exponentially with the help of an experienced attorney.

As we have said multiple times throughout this book "DO NOT TRY THIS AT HOME." There are tons of pitfalls and perils for those trying to obtain an expunction on their own without the help of an attorney. We've said it before and we'll say it now, *do not try a do it yourself expunction.*

The primary problem is "do it yourselfers" can stir up a long dormant and as of yet un-pursued case. In other words, if you go making haphazard inquiries in the wrong case you can arouse prosecutorial interest and fire up an investigation of you and your case/arrest. Thus, use the resource section of our website at www.ultimatesecondchance.com/resources to help find an attorney in your area.

INDIANA

Introduction

In Indiana, the availability of expungement is rather limited. There are other remedies an individual may pursue, including a gubernatorial pardon, which can make obtaining expungement more likely.

The Law in Indiana

Chapter 5 of the Indiana Code of Criminal Law and Procedure, entitled "Expungement of Arrest Records," is in Article 38 entitled "Proceedings Following Dismissal, Verdict, or Finding" outlines the procedures for petitioning for expungement, the eligibility requirements for obtaining an expungement, and the effect an order granting expungement has on a criminal record. The statute is summarized below.

If an individual was arrested but no criminal charges were filed, or all charges were dropped because:

1. They were based on mistaken identity,

2. No offenses were actually committed, or

3. There was a lack of probable cause,

Then the individual may petition the court for

expungement of the records relating to the arrest.

A petitioner must file his or her petition for expungement in the court in which the charges were filed, or the county in which the arrest occurred. The petition must state the date of the arrest, the charge, the arresting agency, the name of the arresting officer, the case number, the individual's date of birth and social security number.

A petitioner must serve a copy of the petition on the arresting agency and the state central repository for records. Any agency that wishes to oppose the expungement must file a notice within 30 days. Upon receiving the petition, the court may decide to grant it, set a date for a hearing on the matter, or deny it if the court finds the petition is insufficient or the individual is not entitled to an expungement. If the court holds a hearing on the matter, the petition will be granted unless the individual is not eligible for expungement, the individual has a record of arrests, or additional charges are pending against the individual.

Eligibility

As stated above, only individuals who never were charged with the criminal offense for which they were arrested or individuals whose charges were dropped because the charges were based on mistaken identity, because no offense was actually committed, or because no probable cause existed are eligible for expungement in

Illinois regardless of the type of offense.

Effect of Expungement

If the court grants the petition for expungement, the law enforcement agency in control of the records must deliver the records to the individual or destroy them within 30 days of the order granting expungement. The state central repository for records may retain information concerning the arrest for criminal history information. However, the statute does not require any changes in any record made at the time of the arrest or in the record of the court in which the charges were filed.

Expungement for Juveniles

Chapter 8, Article 39 of Title 31 of the Indiana Code of Family Law and Juvenile Law, entitled "Expungement of Records Concerning Delinquent Child or Child in Need of Services," outlines the availability of expungement of records regarding offenses committed as a juvenile. The statute is summarized below.

An individual may petition the juvenile court at any time to remove those records regarding the individual's involvement in juvenile court proceedings. In considering whether to grant the petition, the juvenile court may consider a variety of factors, including among other things, the best interests of the child, the nature of the allegations, and the individual's current status. If the petition is granted, the records must be given to the individual or destroyed.

Other Remedies

Chapter 5 of the Indiana Code of Criminal Law and Procedure, which houses the expungement statutes, also contains another remedy available to individuals with criminal convictions. If more than 15 years have passed since the date the individual was discharged from probation or custody, the individual may petition the state police department to limit access to his or her criminal history information. When a petition of this type is filed, the state police department may not release the individual's criminal history to non-criminal justice agencies.

Article V, Section XVII of the Indiana Constitution grants the Governor the power to grant pardons after conviction for all offenses except treason. The Indiana Parole Board has the authority to review requests and submit recommendations to the Governor regarding all pardon applications. Recent Governors have required a five year waiting period after release from probation or parole before an individual may apply for a pardon. Receiving a Governor's pardon is automatic grounds for judicial expungement.

Indiana Parole Board contact information:
(317) 232-5789
Indiana Parole Board
302 W. Washington
IGCS Room E321
Indianapolis, IN 46202

Conclusion

The availability of expungement in the State of Indiana is rather limited. Any conviction at all will cause an individual to be ineligible for the direct relief of expungement. Relief may be found in the form of a Governor's pardon, however, if an individual has received a criminal conviction. The processes of applying for an expungement or pardon can be very lengthy and time consuming. It is best to retain the services of an experienced attorney.

As we have said multiple times throughout this book "DO NOT TRY THIS AT HOME." There are tons of pitfalls and perils for those trying to obtain an expunction on their own without the help of an attorney. We've said it before and we'll say it now, *do not try a do it yourself expunction*.

The primary problem is "do it yourselfers" can stir up a long dormant and as of yet un-pursued case. In other words, if you go making haphazard inquiries in the wrong case you can arouse prosecutorial interest and fire up an investigation of you and your case/arrest. Thus, use the resource section of our website at www.ultimatesecondchance.com/resources to help find an attorney in your area.

IOWA

Introduction

Iowa provides for differing forms of relief from a criminal record: exclusion, expungement, and exoneration in certain circumstances. The statutes are not entirely clear as to the effect of the different forms of relief, but they are available only in limited circumstances.

The Law in Iowa

Section 692.17 of the Iowa Code of Criminal Law and Procedure, entitled "Exclusion," specifies certain circumstances in which criminal history information will not be included in an individual's criminal record. The statute is summarized below.

> Criminal records in a computer system must not include information after an individual has been acquitted or had his or her charges dismissed. Records of acquittals or dismissals due to insanity or mental incompetence in cases involving injury or an attempt to injure another person, however, may be included.

> Criminal records must not include juvenile conviction data after the individual has reached the age of 21, unless the individual was convicted of a serious or aggravated

offense between the ages of 18 and 21.

Section 907.9 of the Iowa Code of Criminal Law and Procedure, entitled "Discharge from Probation," provides for the expungement of criminal record information for individuals who were granted deferred judgment for a criminal conviction and successfully completed probation. Expungement is available only for individuals granted deferred judgment and is not allowed in any other circumstances. The statute is summarized below.

> When the court determines that the purposes of probation have been fulfilled and all fees have been paid including court costs, the court may enter an order discharging an individual from probation. The court will forward a recommendation as to the restoration of the individual's rights to the Governor. If the judgment originally was deferred, the individual's criminal record will be expunged upon discharge. The record will be expunged only in the cases of deferred judgment and not in any other circumstances.

Section 123.46 of the Iowa Code of Public Health, involving public intoxication, makes consumption of alcohol in a public area a simple misdemeanor. The statute further provides that two years after a conviction for public intoxication, the individual may petition to court to exonerate him or her of the conviction if he or she had no other criminal convictions in that time.

Section 692.5 of the Iowa Code of Criminal Law and Procedure, entitled "Right of Notice, Access and Challenge," provides the opportunity for all individuals with criminal records to review their criminal history and challenge the accuracy of their records. The relief can range from simply correcting minor mistakes to complete expungement. The statute is summarized below.

> An individual has the right to obtain a copy of his or her criminal history record. To obtain a copy, the individual must send a written authorization along with a copy of his or her fingerprints to the Department of Public Safety. An individual may request the Department to correct or erase information that is not based on fact or is incorrect. The department will notify the individual of its decision regarding the request within 20 days. If the individual is not satisfied with the department's decision, he or she may file a petition with the court for judicial review.

Eligibility

The type of relief allowed depends on the particular circumstances in the case. Individuals who have been acquitted or had all the charges against them dropped will have the information excluded from their criminal records regardless of the type of offense. The only exception is that the court will retain the criminal records for individuals acquitted or dismissed due to a ruling that they were incompetent to stand trial in cases involving violent crimes.

Expungement is available only for individuals who were granted deferred judgment and successfully completed probation. Exoneration is available only in cases of the simple misdemeanor of public intoxication, but only after two years have passed since the conviction without any other conviction.

Effect of Expungement

The Iowa statutes do not specifically outline the effect of expungement, exclusion or exoneration. It appears the record is not destroyed, however, because the statute states that the information may be used for "management" or "research purposes."

Expungement for Juveniles

The Iowa statutes include juvenile expungement in Section 692.17 of the Iowa Code of Criminal Law and Procedure dealing with exclusions. In most circumstances the criminal history information involving offenses committed as a juvenile will not be included in an individual's criminal record. The statute is summarized below.

> Criminal records must not include juvenile conviction data after the individual has reached the age of 21, unless the individual was convicted of a serious or aggravated offense between the ages of 18 and 21.

Other Remedies

Article IV, Section 16 of the Iowa Constitution grant the Governor the power to grant a full pardon after a criminal conviction. An individual may apply for a pardon through the Iowa Board of Parole or to the Governor directly. An individual may apply for a pardon at any time after a conviction; however, it is the general policy of the Governor's office to require ten years since discharge from the most recent conviction before accepting pardon applications. The Board of Paroles reviews the applications and makes recommendations to the Governor.

Iowa Board of Paroles contact information:

(515) 725-5757
Iowa Board of Parole
510 East 12th St., Suite 3
Des Moines, IA 50319

Conclusion

Although the Iowa statutes allow for individuals to petition on their own for exclusion, expungement, or exoneration, the process can be extremely complex and time consuming. The chance of successfully obtaining relief from a criminal record improves dramatically with the help of an experienced attorney.

As we have said multiple times throughout this book "DO NOT TRY THIS AT HOME." There are tons of pitfalls and perils for those trying to obtain an expunction on their own without the help of an attorney. We've said it before and we'll say it now, ***do not try a do it yourself expunction.***

The primary problem is "do it yourselfers" can stir up a long dormant and as of yet un-pursued case. In other words, if you go making haphazard inquiries in the wrong case you can arouse prosecutorial interest and fire up an investigation of you and your case/arrest. Thus, use the resource section of our website at www.ultimatesecondchance.com/resources to help find an attorney in your area.

KANSAS

Introduction

In Kansas, expungement is available for a wide variety of criminal offenses. The relief of expungement may be available to seal convictions and arrests regardless of the outcome of the case. The type of offense determines the waiting period required before an individual may petition the court for an expungement. Certain offenses, however, are not eligible for expungement.

The Law in Kansas

Section 22-2410 of the Kansas Code of Criminal Procedure outlines the procedure to follow and requirements that must be met in order to petition for expungement. The statute is summarized below.

> An individual who has been arrested may petition the district court for expungement of the record relating to the arrest. The petition must state the individual's full name, sex, race and date of birth, the crime for which he or she was arrested, the date of arrest, and the law enforcement agency that made the arrest. There is no fee for filing the petition.

The court will set a date for a hearing on the petition and notify the prosecuting attorney and law enforcement agency. Anyone with relevant information concerning the individual may testify at the hearing, and the court may look into the background of the individual.

The court will grant an order expunging the record if it finds that:

1. The arrest was due to mistaken identity;

2. There was no probable cause for the arrest;

3. The individual was found not guilty; or

4. The expungement would be in the interests of justice and the charges were dismissed or were never filed.

Section 12-4516 makes expungement available to individuals with certain types of criminal convictions. The statute is summarized below.

An individual who was convicted for the violation of a city ordinance can petition the court for expungement of the conviction if three or more years have elapsed since the individual completed his or her sentence.

Individuals with certain convictions involving vehicular manslaughter, DUI, driving with a suspended license, making a false affidavit, vehicle registration fraud, leaving the scene of an accident, failure to maintain liability insurance, and any felony where a motor vehicle was used in the perpetration of the crime, may not petition for expungement until at least five years have elapsed since the individual completed his or her sentence.

Section 21-4619 of the Kansas Criminal Code is similar to Section 12-4516 of the Code for Municipal Courts except that it adds to the list of criminal offenses for which individuals must wait five years before petitioning for expungement, and it lists offenses that may not be expunged. The statute is summarized below.

An individual convicted of a traffic infraction, cigarette or tobacco infraction, misdemeanor or a Class D or E felony, non-drug crimes ranked in severity levels 6 through 10 or any felony ranked in severity level 4 of the drug grid, may petition the convicting court for expungement if three or more years have elapsed since the individual completed his or her sentence.

Individuals convicted of a Class A, B or C felony, off-grid felonies or any non-drug crime ranked in severity levels 1 through 5 or any felony ranked in severity levels 1 through 3 of the drug grid may not petition for expungement until at least five years have elapsed since the completion of their sentence.

Expungement is not available for convictions involving rape, indecent liberties with a child, criminal sodomy, indecent solicitation of a child, sexual exploitation of a child, aggravated incest, endangering a child, abuse of a child, capital murder, murder in the first degree, murder in the second degree, voluntary manslaughter, involuntary manslaughter, or sexual battery

In both cases, Section 12-4516 and Section 21-4619 require the same procedure for petitioning for expungement. The requirements for these two sections are outlined below.

The petition must state the individual's full name, sex, race and date of birth, the crime for which he or she was arrested, the date of arrest, and the law enforcement agency that made the arrest. There is no fee for filing the petition.

The court will set a date for a hearing on the petition and notify the prosecuting attorney and law enforcement agency. Anyone with relevant information concerning the individual may testify at the hearing, and the court may look into the background of the individual.

The court will grant an order expunging the record if it finds that:

1. The individual has not been convicted of a felony in the past two years and no charges are pending;

2. The circumstances warrant expungement; and

3. Expungement is consistent with the public welfare.

Eligibility

Convictions for a wide variety of offenses may be expunged according to the Kansas statute. Some types of offenses may require a longer waiting period before petitioning for expungement than other offenses. An individual who has been acquitted or who never was charged with an offense, regardless of the type of offense, may petition for expungement without waiting. Expungement is not available for convictions involving rape, indecent liberties with a child, criminal sodomy, indecent solicitation of a child, sexual exploitation of a child, aggravated incest, endangering a child, aggravated endangering a child, abuse of a child, capital murder, murder in the first degree, murder in the second degree, voluntary manslaughter, involuntary manslaughter, or sexual battery

Effect of Expungement

In Kansas, expungement means the sealing of records. The records are not available except to the individual to which the records relate and criminal justice agencies. If a court enters an order for expungement, the individual is treated as if he or she never was arrested or convicted. If records were expunged after a conviction, the records may be released to certain private employment agencies on a limited basis. The court will make the information available in applications for certain types of private employment, applications to practice law in the state, applications for employment with the Kansas Lottery or Racing Commission, applications for a commercial driver's license, applications for a concealed handgun permit and any other circumstances the court feels appropriate. In those circumstances the individual must acknowledge the expunged conviction, but he or she is not required to do so in any other employment context. Also, if the records were expunged after a conviction, upon any subsequent conviction, the expunged conviction may be considered in determining the sentence to be imposed.

Expungement for Juveniles

Section 38-1608 of the Kansas Juvenile Justice Code requires that records concerning a public offense committed by a juvenile under the age of 14 be kept separate from criminal and other records and are not be disclosed to anyone except the judge and members of the court, parties to the proceedings, the Department of Social and Rehabilitative

Services, and certain other government agencies.

Other Remedies

Article 1, Section 7 of the Kansas Constitution gives the Governor the power to grant pardons for all types of criminal convictions. The Kansas Parole Board is responsible for reviewing all application for executive clemency and making recommendations to the Governor.

Kansas Parole Board contact information:

(785) 296-3469
Kansas Parole Board
Landon State Office Building
900 S.W. Jackson, 4th Floor
Topeka, KS 66612

Conclusion

Although Kansas makes expungement available in a wide variety of circumstances, the ability to successfully obtain an order granting expungement depends primarily on how effectively you can argue your case to the judge during your hearing. The chances of obtaining the relief of expungement in the State of Kansas greatly increase with the assistance of an experienced attorney.

As we have said multiple times throughout this book "DO NOT TRY THIS AT HOME." There are tons of pitfalls and perils for those trying to obtain an expunction on their own without the help of an attorney. We've said it before and we'll say it now, ***do not try a do it yourself expunction.***

The primary problem is "do it yourselfers" can stir up a long dormant and as of yet un-pursued case. In other words, if you go making haphazard inquiries in the wrong case you can arouse prosecutorial interest and fire up an investigation of you and your case/arrest. Thus, use the resource section of our website at www.ultimatesecondchance.com/resources to help find an attorney in your area.

KENTUCKY

Introduction

In Kentucky, expungement is available in limited circumstances. The statutes outline specific requirements an individual must satisfy in order to be eligible for expungement. Generally only misdemeanor convictions may be expunged, however, there are a few exceptions embedded within the statutes.

The Law in Kentucky

Section 431.076 of the Kentucky Code of Crimes and Punishments provides for the expungement of criminal records relating to any offense for which an individual was found not guilty or where all charges against the individual were dismissed with prejudice. This section does not apply to cases where all charges were dropped because of a plea agreement. The law is summarized below.

> An individual who was charged with a criminal offense but found not guilty or had all charges against him or her dismissed with prejudice may make a motion in the court in which the charges were filed to expunge all records arising out of the arrest or charge.

> The motion may not be filed until 60 days pass

following the order of acquittal or dismissal. Upon receiving the motion, the court may set a date for a hearing and notify the county or state attorney. If the court finds that there are no current proceedings pending concerning the matter, the court may grant the motion and order the sealing of all records.

In the case of a conviction, Section 431.078 of the Kentucky Code of Crimes and Punishment entitled Expungement of Misdemeanor and Violation Conviction Records allows for expungement of records for misdemeanor or violation convictions. The law is summarized below.

An individual who has been convicted of a misdemeanor or violation may petition the court which convicted him or her for expungement of his or her record. The petition may not be filed until five years have passed since the completion of the individual's sentence or probation.

Upon receiving the petition, the court will set a date for a hearing and notify the county attorney, the victim of the crime, and any other person with relevant information regarding the expungement of the record.

The judge will issue an order to seal the records relating to the offense if he or she finds that:

1. The offense was not a sex offense or an offense against a child;

2. The individual had no previous felony convictions;

3. The individual had no misdemeanor or violation convictions in the five years prior to the conviction;

4. The individual had not been convicted of a felony, misdemeanor, or violation since the time of the conviction;

5. No felony, misdemeanor, or violation proceedings are pending against the individual; and

6. The offense was against the Commonwealth of Kentucky.

Eligibility

In Kentucky, an individual may petition the court to expunge his or her criminal record if he or she was found not guilty of the offense or all charges against him or her were dismissed. An individual may also petition the court to expunge misdemeanor and violation convictions provided he or she meets all of the requirements set forth in the statute. The only felonies eligible for expungement are Class D drug possession convictions.

The Effect of Expungement

After the court enters an order to seal the records, the proceedings are deemed never to have occurred. The individual may then reply that no record exists upon any inquiry into the matter. The individual does not have to disclose the fact of the record on any type of application, including any job applications the individual may fill out. Inspection of the record is permitted only upon petition by the individual who is the subject of the records.

Expungement for Juveniles

Section 610.340 of the Kentucky Unified Juvenile Code, entitled "Confidentiality of Juvenile Court Records," extends certain disclosure limitations to all Juvenile Court Records. The records may only be obtained by a certain, limited group of individuals. Section 610.330 of the Kentucky Unified Juvenile Code, entitled "Expungement of Juvenile Court Records," provides further relief for juvenile offenders and allows for the expungement of criminal records for certain types of juvenile offenses after a specified period of time has elapsed. The statue is summarized below.

> Any child who was convicted of a status offense, misdemeanor, or violation may petition the court to expunge his juvenile record. If the offense would have been a felony when committed by an adult, it may not be expunged. The petition may not be filed until two years have passed since the termination of the court's jurisdiction over the individual. The two-year period may be waived by the court in extraordinary circumstances.
>
> Upon receiving the petition, the court will set a date for a hearing and notify the county attorney and anyone else with relevant information concerning the expungement. The judge will order all records sealed if at the hearing the he or she finds that:
>
> 1. The individual has not been convicted of a felony in the two years since the termination of the court's jurisdiction; and
>
> 2. No felony proceedings are pending against him or her.

Lesser Remedies

Section 77 of the Kentucky Constitution grants the Governor the broad authority to grant pardons for criminal offenses. A pardon makes a conviction a legal nullity, but it is not the same as an expungement and barring extraordinary circumstances, a pardon will not remove a case from the public court files. The Governor requires a 7 year waiting period before and individual becomes eligible to receive a pardon. Pardon applications are made to the Kentucky Parole board, who then forward their recommendations on to the Governor.

Kentucky Parole Board contact information:

> (502) 564-3620
> Kentucky Parole Board
> Post Office Box 2400
> Frankfort, KY 40602

Conclusion

In Kentucky, expungement is granted only if all statutory requirements have been meet. The process of petitioning for expungement can be complex and time consuming. As always, the chances of successfully obtaining an order grating expungement improve dramatically with the help of an experienced attorney.

As we have said multiple times throughout this book, "DO NOT TRY THIS AT HOME." There are tons of pitfalls and perils for those trying to obtain an expunction on their own without the help of an attorney. We've said it before and we'll say it now, ***do not try a do it yourself expungement.***

The primary problem is "do it yourselfers" can stir up a long dormant and as of yet un-pursued case. In other words, if you go making haphazard inquiries in the wrong case you can arouse prosecutorial interest and fire up an investigation of you and your case/arrest. Thus, use the resource section of our website at www.ultimatesecondchance.com/resources to help find an attorney in your area.

LOUISIANA

Introduction

In Louisiana, the statutes provide a variety of situations where expungement may be used as a form of relief from the negative effects of a criminal record. Expungement is available when an individual is acquitted of an offense and also when all charges against the individual are dismissed. Dismissal can be due to a variety of reasons, including the completion of probation.

The Law in Louisiana

Title 44, Section 9 of the Louisiana Statutes outlines the requirements that must be met in order to obtain expungement for certain misdemeanor and felony offenses. The statute is summarized below.

> Any individual who was arrested for the violation of a municipal ordinance or state misdemeanor may make a written motion to the court for expungement of the record, if either:
>
> > 1. The time limitation for prosecution has expired, and no prosecution was instituted; or

2. All proceedings were disposed of by dismissal or acquittal.

If the court determines that the individual is entitled to expungement, the court will order all agencies to destroy records of the arrest.

An individual who has been arrested for a felony offense may make a request that the court expunge the record if:

1. The time limitation for prosecution has expired, and no prosecution was instituted; or

2. All proceedings were disposed of by acquittal or dismissal; and

3. The record will not be of value in any later prosecution.

If, after a hearing, the court determines that the individual is entitled to expungement, the court will order all agencies to expunge the record.

The court may not order the record destroyed in felony or DUI cases, and the record still may be considered in future prosecution and by government agencies.

Title 44, Section 9 also establishes that individuals who receive deferred sentences for felony and misdemeanor convictions and are placed on probation pursuant to Articles 893 and 894 of the Louisiana Code of Criminal Procedure are eligible for expungement. The court grants deferred sentencing in limited circumstances and probation must be completed and all prosecution dismissed before an individual is eligible to seek expungement. The criminal records in such instances are not destroyed, but are stored confidentially and may be accessed only by certain government agencies.

Eligibility

Louisiana provides for a variety of circumstances in which expungement may be an available form of relief from the haunting effects of a criminal record. Expungement is available for both misdemeanor and felony offenses, including DUI offenses, that were dismissed due to an individual's successful completion of a probationary program. Expungement is not available for the criminal records of sex offenses involving children under the age of 17.

Effect of Expungement

In Louisiana, expungement means the removal of a record from public access, but it does not mean the destruction of the record. Expunged records are confidential, and they are available for use only by certain law enforcement and government agencies. After the entry of an order of expungement, all rights which were lost due to a conviction are restored to the individual and he or she shall be treated as not having been arrested or convicted. The individual is not required to disclose he or she was ever arrested or convicted unless he or she is seeking employment or licensure from certain government agencies.

Expungement for Juveniles

Chapter 18 of Title VIII of Article 917 of the Louisiana Children's Code establishes the relief of expungement for juvenile records. Article 918 lists the grounds for expungement, Article 919 outlines the procedure an individual must follow in order to obtain an order granting expungement, and Articles 20 and 21 specify the effect of an order granting expungement has on juvenile records. The statutes are summarized below.

Once an individual reaches the age of 17, he or she may move the court for the expungement of his or her juvenile records. The motion must be in writing and state the grounds for expungement. Expungement is available only in the following situations:

1. The records relate to conduct that did not result in a conviction;

2. The records relate to a misdemeanor conviction and two years have elapsed since the termination of the sentence; or

3. The records relate to felony conviction and:

a. The conviction did not involve murder, manslaughter, sexual offenses, kidnapping, or armed robbery;

b. Five years have elapsed since the termination of the sentence;

c. The individual has no convictions involving a weapon; and

d. The individual has no pending charges against him or her.

The motion must be served upon the district attorney, the court clerk, and the head of the law enforcement agency. The court will conduct a hearing. If the court finds proper grounds and feels the individual is entitled to relief, the court will grant an order for expungement, in which case all records are destroyed. Undestroyed records may not be released.

Other Remedies

Article 4, Section 5 of the Louisiana Constitution gives the Governor the power to grant pardons for criminal convictions. The Louisiana Board of Pardons reviews pardon applications and forwards recommendations to the Governor.

Louisiana Board of Pardons contact information:

(225) 342-5421
Pardon Board
504 Mayflower St.
Building 6
Baton Rouge, LA 70802

Conclusion

In Louisiana, several situations exist in which an individual may be eligible to seek an order from the court granting the expungement of a criminal record. The process of requesting an expungement can be complex and time consuming, and the likelihood of successfully obtaining an order of expungement greatly increases with the help of an experienced attorney.

As we have said multiple times throughout this book "DO NOT TRY THIS AT HOME." There are tons of pitfalls and perils for those trying to obtain an expunction on their own without the help of an attorney. We've said it before and we'll say it now, *do not try a do it yourself expungement.*

The primary problem is "do it yourselfers" can stir up a long dormant and as of yet un-pursued case. In other words, if you go making haphazard inquiries in the wrong case you can arouse prosecutorial interest

and fire up an investigation of you and your case/arrest. Thus, use the resource section of our website at www.ultimatesecondchance.com/resources to help find an attorney in your area.

MAINE

Introduction

Maine is one of the few states that does not allow for expungement of criminal history record information. Despite this fact, alternative means of relief for individuals may exist in the form of a pardon or the sealing of records.

The Law in Maine

Maine does not explicitly allow for the expungement of criminal history information. Title 16, Chapter 3, Subchapter 8, entitled "The Criminal History Record Information Act," divides criminal history information into two categories: conviction data and nonconviction data. The ability to access the information contained in the criminal record depends on whether the information is considered conviction data or nonconviction data. The Act is summarized below.

Nonconviction data includes the following types of information:

1. Arrest information if one year has passed since the date of the arrest and no prosecution is pending;

2. Information that the police have elected

not to refer the matter for prosecution;

3. Information that the prosecutor has elected not to proceed with the charges;

4. Information that proceedings have been postponed or that a case cannot be tried because the individual is mentally incompetent;

5. A dismissal;

6. An acquittal unless it is for reasons of mental disease or defect; and

7. Information that an individual has received a full pardon or amnesty.

The dissemination of nonconviction data is limited and may be received only by criminal justice agencies, individuals with the express authorization of a court order, individuals under specific agreements to provide services to a criminal justice agency, and individuals conducting statistical research.

All other criminal history information is considered conviction data and may be disseminated to any person for any purpose. No matter the type of data, however, an individual may request amendment or correction of criminal record information concerning him or her by sending a request to the criminal justice agency in charge of the record. The request must indicate the record involved and the nature and justification for the correction.

Eligibility

Because Maine does not allow for the expungement of criminal history record information, only nonconviction information is protected from public dissemination.

The Effect of Expungement

Maine does not allow for the expungement of criminal history record information, and all conviction records may be disseminated to any person for any purpose. If the criminal history relates to offenses for which there was no conviction, the data is maintained by the criminal justice agency, but access to the information is strictly limited.

Sealing of Records for Juveniles

Maine allows a bit more relief for juveniles convicted of criminal offenses. Only certain, limited individuals may obtain copies of juvenile records, and in many cases, an individual may have his or her juvenile record sealed. Section 3308 of the Maine Juvenile Code (petition, adjudication, and disposition) outlines the limitations on the dissemination of juvenile records and the possible sealing of such records. The statute is summarized below.

Maine limits the dissemination of juvenile criminal records and the records may be inspected only in certain circumstances. If a juvenile hearing is open to the public, the records are open to public inspection. The records of the proceedings also may be inspected by the parties, any agency that has custody of the juvenile, the Department of Health and Human Services, criminal justice agencies, and individuals who have court permission. The name of a juvenile is only disclosed to the victim of the crime and the Victim Compensation Board.

If the offense involves certain types of criminal activity, the records may be disseminated on a broader scale. When the crime involves the operation of a motor vehicle, the records are sent to the Secretary of State and are open to public inspection. If the juvenile has been convicted of a juvenile crime, the information may be inspected by the juvenile's supervisors and the superintendent of the juvenile's school. If a juvenile is convicted of a juvenile crime that would be gross sexual assault if committed by an adult, the Department of Corrections must provide copies of the records to all licensed day-care facility operators where the juvenile lives, and any other agencies the Department feels appropriate.

An individual convicted of a juvenile crime may petition the court to seal all juvenile records if:

1. Three years have passed since the individual's discharge;

2. The juvenile has not been convicted of another juvenile crime in that time; and

3. There are no charges pending against the juvenile.

The court will seal the records if it finds that all the requirements are satisfied unless the public's right to the information substantially outweighs the juvenile's interest in the sealing of records. Sealed records may be accessed only by the court and criminal justice agencies and the individual who is the subject of the records. Once the record has been sealed, the juvenile may answer that he or she has never been convicted of a crime upon direct inquiry.

Other Remedies

Article 5, Section 11 of the Maine Constitution gives the Governor the power to grant pardons for most convictions. The Secretary of State receives and reviews applications and may grant a hearing before the Division of Probation and Parole of the Department of Corrections. The Department will make a recommendation to the Governor regarding the pardon application and hearing, but the Governor retains the ultimate decision making power whether to grant a pardon. An individual is eligible to apply for a pardon after five years have passed since the completion of his or her sentence. Once a pardon is granted, the record becomes nonconviction data subject to strict limitations on dissemination.

Maine Pardon Board contact information:

> (207) 624-7650
> Pardon Clerk
> Office of the Secretary of State
> 101 State House Station
> Augusta, ME 04333

Conclusion

Although expungement is not available in Maine, options for sealing a criminal record still exist for juveniles. Pardons also are possible sources of relief from the haunting effects of a criminal record. Maine grants fewer pardons then most states, and the chances of successfully receiving such relief greatly improve with the help of an experienced attorney.

As we have said multiple times throughout this book "DO NOT TRY THIS AT HOME." There are tons of pitfalls and perils for those trying to obtain relief from a criminal record on their own without the help of an attorney. We've said it before and we'll say it now, *do not try a do it yourself expunction*.

The primary problem is "do it yourselfers" can stir up a long dormant and as of yet un-pursued case. In other words, if you go making haphazard inquiries in the wrong case you can arouse prosecutorial interest and fire up an investigation of you and your case/arrest. Thus, use the resource section of our website at www.ultimatesecondchance.com/resources to help find an attorney in your area.

MARYLAND

Introduction

Maryland provides many opportunities for individuals looking to clear their criminal records. The Maryland statutes regarding expungement are very precise, and the Maryland Rules even contain the forms necessary to apply for expungement.

The Law in Maryland

Sections 10-101 through 10-109 of the Maryland Code of Criminal Procedure (expungement of police and court records) outline the availability and effect of the expungement of criminal records. Several Maryland Rules parallel the statutes and contain forms to complete and procedures to follow when applying for an expungement. The statutes are summarized below.

An individual who is arrested and released without being charged with a crime may request the expungement of the record by filing an application for expungement with the law enforcement agency. The application can be found at Form 4-503.3 of the Appendix of Forms to the Maryland Rules. The individual may not request expungement until the statute of limitations has run for all tort claims that arise from the incident unless the application is accompanied by a general waiver and release of all claims. An application must be filed within eight years of the date of the arrest.

When the law enforcement agency receives the application, it will investigate the claims and expunge the record if the facts in the application are true. The agency will send a verification of the facts and expungement to the individual making the request. If the request for expungement is denied, the individual may apply for an order of expungement from the district court. The court will notify the law enforcement agency and will conduct a hearing on the matter. If the court finds the individual is eligible for expungement, the court will grant the request.

Section 10-105 of the Maryland Code of Criminal Procedure, entitled "Expungement of Record after Charge is Filed," outlines the process of applying for an expungement where charges actually were filed. The statute is summarized below.

An individual who has been charged with a crime may file a petition for the expungement of the record in the following circumstances:

1. The individual was acquitted;

2. The charge was dismissed;

3. A probation before judgment was entered, unless the offense involved

driving under the influence or kidnapping;

4. A *nolle prosequi* or *nolle prosequi* with the requirement of drug or alcohol treatment was entered;

5. The court indefinitely postponed the trial by marking the charge "stet" or stet with the requirement of drug or alcohol abuse treatment;

6. The charge was transferred to the juvenile court; or

7. The individual was convicted of only one, non-violent crime and received a full and unconditional pardon from the Governor.

The individual must file a petition in the court where the proceeding began. The petition can be found at Form 4-504.1 of the Appendix of Forms to the Maryland Rules. The court will send a copy of the petition to the State's Attorney, and unless the State's Attorney files an objection to the petition, the court will order the expungement of all police and court records relating to the charge. If the State's Attorney files an objection, the court will conduct a hearing on the matter to determine whether the individual is entitled to expungement and will grant or deny the request.

Eligibility

A police record or court record may be expunged if no charges were filed or charges were filed and the individual was acquitted, the charges were dismissed, the individual was granted probation before judgment, and a few other instances outlined above. When charges are filed, depending on the nature of the disposition, the individual may have to wait a certain number of years before becoming eligible to petition for expungement. In any conviction requiring drug or alcohol abuse treatment, the individual must first complete all of the treatment before becoming eligible to petition for expungement. A court, in its discretion may, however, grant expungement at any time. If an individual is charged with two or more crimes arising out of the same incident and is not entitled to expungement of one of the charges, he or she is not entitled to expungement for any of the charges. Minor traffic violations are not eligible for expungement.

Effect of Expungement

After the court grants an order of expungement, all records are to be sealed and sequestered in a locked file. Sealed records may be unsealed with a court order, and the court may allow access to the records in the interest of justice. The sealed records are to be retained for a minimum of three years and may be destroyed after three years have passed.

Expungement for Juveniles

Like many states, Maryland offers greater protection to juvenile offenders. Section 3-8A-27 of the Maryland Code of Courts and Judicial Proceedings, entitled "Privacy of Records," outlines the strict confidentiality requirements concerning the records of juvenile offenders. The statute is summarized below.

Police records concerning juveniles are confidential and kept separate from adult records. The contents of juvenile records may be released only by court order. The Department of Juvenile Services or any law enforcement agency may access the records in the investigation or prosecution of the juvenile.

The court, on its own motion or on petition, can order the court records of the juvenile sealed, and the records must be sealed after the juvenile reaches the age of 21. Once the records are sealed, they may not be opened except by court order.

Section 10-106 of the Maryland Code of Criminal Procedure, entitled "Expungement of Criminal Charge Transferred to Juvenile Court," provides that individuals charged or adjudicated as juvenile delinquents may petition for expungement.

The court may grant expungement of a charge transferred to the juvenile court that resulted in the adjudication of the individual as a delinquent child to a juvenile after he or she reaches the age of 21.

The court must grant a petition for expungement if the charge did not result in the filing of a delinquency petition or the petition resulted in a finding of facts-not-sustained. An individual may file a petition for expungement of a criminal charge transferred to the juvenile court after the date of a decision not to file a delinquency charge or a decision of facts-not-sustained. The petition can be found in Maryland Rule 11-601.

Other Remedies

Section 20 of the Maryland Constitution gives the Governor the power to grant full and unconditional pardons for most criminal convictions. The Maryland Parole Commission reviews pardon applications and makes recommendation thereon to the Governor who then decides whether to grant the requested pardons. An individual will be eligible for expungement five years after receiving a full and unconditional pardon from the Governor.

Maryland Parole Commission contact information:

> (410) 585-3500
> Pardon Application
> Maryland Parole Commission
> 6776 Reisterstown Road, Suite 307
> Baltimore, MD 21215-2343

Conclusion

Maryland provides many opportunities for individuals to clear their criminal records. The processes involved in obtaining expungement or pardon can be complex and time consuming. The chances of successfully clearing a criminal records increase dramatically with the help of an experienced attorney.

As we have said multiple times throughout this book "DO NOT TRY THIS AT HOME." There are tons of pitfalls and perils for those trying to obtain an expunction on their own without the help of an attorney. We've said it before and we'll say it now, *do not try a do it yourself expunction.*

The primary problem is "do it yourselfers" can stir up a long dormant and as of yet un-pursued case. In other words, if you go making haphazard inquiries in the wrong case you can arouse prosecutorial interest and fire up an investigation of you and your case/arrest. Thus, use the resource section of our website at www.ultimatesecondchance.com/resources to help find an attorney in your area.

MASSACHUSETTS

Introduction

The Massachusetts statutes recognize both expungement and sealing of records relating to criminal offenses. The ability to grant expungement is considered an implied power of the courts recognized by the legislature. The statutes, however, make it relatively clear that the sealing of records is the more appropriate form of relief in most circumstances, and may be available even in the event of an actual conviction.

The Law in Massachusetts

Chapter 276, Section 100C of the Massachusetts General Laws requires the sealing of criminal records in cases where an individual is found not guilty or the charges are dismissed. The statute is outlined below.

> In a criminal case where the defendant was found not guilty, the grand jury returned no bill, or no probable cause existed, the Commissioner of Probation must seal all the records relating to the case.

> In a criminal case that results in *nolle prosequi* or dismissal and it appears to the court that

justice would be served, the court will order the records of the proceeding sealed.

Chapter 276, Section 100A of the Massachusetts General Laws outlines the procedure that individuals seeking sealing of their criminal records must follow and the requirements they must meet. The Commissioner of Probation provides forms for making such requests. The statute is summarized below.

> An individual with a criminal record can file a form provided by the commissioner of probation and signed under penalties of perjury requesting that the commissioner seal the records.
>
> The commissioner will seal the records if the following conditions are met:

1. If the crime was a misdemeanor, the individual's court appearance, disposition, or completion of sentence occurred more than ten years before the request was made;

2. If the crime was a felony, the individual's court appearance, disposition, or completion of sentence occurred more than 15 years before the request was made;

3. The individual has not been found guilty of any other criminal offense in the time between the completion of the sentence and the time of the

request, except for motor vehicle offenses with a
penalty not exceeding a fine of $50;

4. The request form includes a statement by the
    individual that he or she has not been convicted of
    a criminal offense in another state and has not
    been imprisoned in another state within the
    preceding ten years; and

5. The individual's record does not include a
    conviction for certain offenses involving the illegal
    sale of firearms, crimes against public justice, or an
    illegal act while serving as a public official or
    employee.

Section 44 of the Controlled Substances Act pertains
specifically to the sealing of records for crimes involving the
illegal possession of a controlled substance. The Section
allows for the sealing of court records, but not police
records. The statute is summarized below.

If an individual is found not guilty of the
unlawful possession of a controlled substance,
the complaint is dismissed, or an indictment
nol prossed for such violation, the court will
order all the court records sealed. However,
the departmental, non-public records kept by
law enforcement will not be sealed.

According to Massachusetts case law, the
expungement of adult criminal records generally is
permitted only in cases where an individual's identity was

stolen and, as a result, the records are inaccurate.

Eligibility

The statutes providing for the sealing of a criminal record outline the specific eligibility requirements for individuals looking to seal their criminal records. An individual may be eligible to have his or her record sealed even if he or she was convicted of a felony or misdemeanor. In the event of an actual conviction, the statutes require a waiting period, depending on the nature of the crime, before an individual becomes eligible to request his or her records sealed. The sealing of records is not available in cases where the order of probation has been terminated.

Effect of Expungement

After criminal records are sealed, they are segregated from all other criminal records that have not been sealed. Sealed records may not disqualify an individual from public or private employment. In any application for employment, the individual may respond that he or she has no record upon a direct inquiry. The records are not destroyed, however, and sealed records may be admissible as evidence in subsequent criminal proceedings. If, in the rare event the records are ordered expunged, they are physically destroyed.

Expungement for Juveniles

Massachusetts, like most other states, affords greater protection and confidentiality to the criminal records of juvenile offenders. Chapter 119, Section 60A of the Massachusetts General Laws establishes the extent to which juvenile records are open for public inspection. The statute is summarized below.

> The criminal records of juvenile offenders who were indicted are open to public inspection in the same manner as adult criminal court records. All other juvenile records must be withheld from public inspection except with the consent of the court.

> The name of the juvenile is available to the public if the juvenile is alleged to have committed an offense between the ages of 14 and 17, and he or she has been convicted at least two times prior to the current offense for acts which would have been punishable by imprisonment in the state prison if the juvenile had been age 17 or older.

Chapter 276, Section 100B outlines the eligibility requirements and procedures that an individual seeking to have his or her juvenile records sealed must follow. The statute is summarized below.

> An individual with a juvenile record can file a form provided by the Commissioner of Probation and signed under penalties of perjury requesting that the commissioner seal the records.

The commissioner will seal the records if the following conditions are met:

1. The juvenile's court appearance, disposition, or completion of sentence occurred more than three years before the request was made;

2. The juvenile has not been found guilty of any other criminal offense in the time between the completion of his or her sentence and when the request was made, except for motor vehicle offenses with a penalty not exceeding a fine of $50; and

3. The request form includes a statement by the juvenile that he or she has not been convicted of a criminal offense in another state and has not been imprisoned in another state.

According to case law, a court may exercise its power to order expungement of records in juvenile cases if use of the records for law enforcement purposes is minimal or nonexistent.

Other Remedies

Massachusetts Constitution, Part 2, Chapter II, Section I, Article VIII, gives the Governor the power to grant pardons for criminal convictions with the advice and consent of the Governor's Council. All petitions requesting a pardon must be filed with the Massachusetts Parole Board and may not be filed until at least 15 years have elapsed since the conviction or release from prison in felony cases and at least ten years have elapsed since conviction or release in misdemeanor cases.

Massachusetts Parole Board contact information:

(978) 740-6488
Massachusetts Parole Board/Advisory Board of Pardons
P.O. Box 4547
Salem, MA 01970

Conclusion

In Massachusetts, the statutes provide that criminal records may be sealed in a wide variety of circumstances. Even after a felony conviction, an individual may be eligible to have his or her records sealed. The process of obtaining an order granting the sealing of records can be complex and should be accomplished with the help of an experienced attorney.

As we have said multiple times throughout this book "DO NOT TRY THIS AT HOME." There are tons of pitfalls and perils for those trying to obtain an expunction on their own without the help of an attorney. We've said it before and we'll say it now, ***do not try a do it yourself expunction.***

The primary problem is "do it yourselfers" can stir up a long dormant and as of yet un-pursued case. In other words, if you go making haphazard inquiries in the wrong case you can arouse prosecutorial interest

and fire up an investigation of you and your case/arrest. Thus, use the resource section of our website at www.ultimatesecondchance.com/resources to help find an attorney in your area.

MICHIGAN

Introduction

In Michigan, the statutes provide for the expungement of criminal records in the form of an order setting aside a criminal conviction. Most types of criminal convictions may be set aside if an individual meets all the statutory requirements. A few certain types of convictions, however, are exempt from set-aside eligibility.

The Law in Michigan

Section 780.612 of the Michigan Code of Criminal Procedure provides individuals the opportunity to request that the court set aside a criminal conviction and outlines the procedure for making such a request. The statute is summarized below.

An individual who has only ever been convicted of one criminal offense may file an application with the court requesting an order to set aside the conviction. The individual may not file the application for set-aside until five years has passed since the completion of the sentence. The application must be signed under oath by the individual seeking a set-aside, and the application must contain the following information:

1. The individual's full name and address;

2. A certified record of the conviction the individual is seeking to set aside.

3. A statement that the individual has never been convicted of any other offense;

4. A statement concerning whether the individual has filed for a set-aside before and the results of that application;

5. A statement concerning whether the individual has any other charges pending against him or her; and

6. A statement consenting to the access of the non-public record.

The individual must send the application to the Department of State Police along with two complete sets of fingerprints and $50.00 payable to the State of Michigan. The department will investigate the facts in the application and report the information to the court.

A copy of the application is also sent to the attorney general and the prosecuting attorney who have the opportunity to contest the application. If the conviction involved an assault or serious misdemeanor, the prosecuting attorney will notify the victim of the crime. The victim has the right to appear at any proceeding related to the set-aside and make a statement.

The court will conduct a hearing on the application. If the court determines that, based on the circumstances of the case, the individual deserves to have his or her conviction set-aside and that setting aside the conviction is consistent with the public welfare, the court will enter an order setting aside the conviction.

Eligibility

To be eligible to have a conviction set aside, an individual may only have ever been convicted of one criminal offense. The statute also exempts certain crimes from set-aside eligibility. Felony convictions for which the maximum punishment is life in prison, convictions for criminal sexual conduct, and convictions for traffic offenses may not be set-aside.

Effect of Expungement

Once an order setting aside a conviction has been granted, the fingerprint and arrest card relating to the conviction that was set aside must be returned to the individual who was granted the set-aside or destroyed. The record may not be made available to any licensing agency of the State.

Expungement for Juveniles

Section of 712.18e of the Michigan Probate Code, entitled "Order Setting Aside Adjudication," provides the opportunity for individuals to request the set aside of juvenile adjudications. The statute is strikingly similar to the set-aside statute for adults. The statute is summarized below.

An individual who has only ever been convicted of one juvenile offense and who has no felony convictions may file an application with the court requesting an order to set aside the conviction. The individual may not file the application for set-aside until five years has passed since the completion of the sentence or when the individual reaches the age of 24, whichever occurs later. The application must be signed under oath by the individual seeking a set-aside, and the application must contain the following information:

1. The individual's full name and address;

2. A certified record of the conviction the individual is seeking to set aside.

3. A statement that the individual has never been convicted of any other juvenile offense;

4. A statement that the individual has never been convicted of a felony offense.

5. A statement concerning whether the individual has filed for a set-aside before and the results of that application;

6. A statement concerning whether the individual has any other charges pending against him or her; and

7. A statement consenting to the access of the non-public record.

The individual must send the application to the department of state police along with two complete sets of fingerprints and $25.00

payable to the State of Michigan. The Department of State Police will investigate the facts in the application and report the information to the court.

A copy of the application is also sent to the attorney general and the prosecuting attorney who have the opportunity to contest the application. If the conviction involved an assault or serious misdemeanor, the prosecuting attorney will notify the victim of the crime. The victim has the right to appear at any proceeding related to the set-aside and make a statement.

The court will conduct a hearing on the application. If the court determines that, based on the circumstances of the case, the individual deserves to have his or her conviction set-aside and that setting aside the conviction is consistent with the public welfare, the court will enter an order setting aside the conviction.

The following juvenile offenses are not eligible for set aside:

1. An offense that if committed by an adult would be a felony for which the maximum punishment is life imprisonment;

2. A felony or misdemeanor offense that

involves the operation of a vehicle;

Lesser Remedies

Article V, Section 14 of the Michigan Constitution gives the Governor the power to grant pardons for criminal convictions. Receiving a pardon from the Governor will restore many of the rights lost due to a criminal conviction. Applications for pardon are to be filed with the Michigan Parole Board. The Board conducts an investigation and hearing into the matter then recommends a course of action to the Governor.

Michigan Parole Board contact information:

> (517) 373-6391
> Michigan Department of Corrections
> Office of the Parole Board
> Pardon and Commutations Coordinator
> P.O. Box 30003
> Lansing, MI 48909

Conclusion

In Michigan, expungement is offered in the form of a set-aside, and set-aside is only available for the convictions of one-time offenders. Applying for the set-aside of a criminal conviction can be extremely complex and is most effective with the help of an experienced attorney.

As we have said multiple times throughout this book "DO NOT TRY THIS AT HOME." There are tons of pitfalls and perils for those trying to obtain an expunction on their own without the help of an attorney. We've said it before and we'll say it now, ***do not try a do it yourself expunction.***

The primary problem is "do it yourselfers" can stir up a long dormant and as of yet un-pursued case. In other words, if you go making haphazard inquiries in the wrong case you can arouse prosecutorial interest and fire up an investigation of you and your case/arrest. Thus, use the resource section of our website at www.ultimatesecondchance.com/resources to help find an attorney in your area.

MINNESOTA

Introduction

In Minnesota, an individual may obtain expungement in limited circumstances. Individuals who were charged with a criminal offense, but never convicted, are eligible for expungement. Also, certain, limited types of criminal convictions may be expunged. Expunged records are not destroyed; rather, the records are sealed and may be accessed only by law enforcement personnel.

The Law in Minnesota

Chapter 690A of the Minnesota Statutes, entitled "Expungement," provides the grounds and procedure for expungement of criminal records. When an expungement order is granted, the records are sealed but not destroyed. The Chapter is summarized below.

An individual looking to expunge his or her criminal record must file a petition and pay a statutory filing fee of $240. The petitioner must sign the petition under oath and provide the following:

1. The individual's full name and any other name by which he or she may be known at the time;

2. The individual's date of birth;

3. All of the individual's addresses from the date of the offense to the date of the petition;

4. The reasons the individual is seeking and why the court should grant the petition;

5. Details of the offense to be expunged;

6. The steps the individual has taken toward rehabilitation since the time of the offense;

7. The individual's criminal conviction records;

8. All prior requests by the individual for expungement.

The individual also must attach any protective or restraining orders against him or her to the petition.

The individual must mail the petition and a proposed expungement order to the office responsible for prosecution against him or her and all other government agencies whose records would be affected by expungement.

The court will conduct a hearing, and victims of the offense have the right to make a statement at that time.

The court will grant expungement only when it determines by clear and convincing evidence that expungement would benefit the individual more so or equal to the disadvantages of sealing the record and the burden imposed on authorities to enforce it.

Eligibility

Only certain types of convictions may be eligible for expungement. Individuals placed on probation without judgment for possession of a controlled substance in the fourth degree, fifth degree, or other controlled substances offense may petition for the sealing of records after the successful completion of probation and the dismissal of all charges against them. Juveniles certified and prosecuted as adults may petition for the sealing of criminal records if the juvenile has been finally discharged by the commissioner or has been discharged after successfully completing probation. A conviction which requires registration as a predatory offender may not be expunged.

Individuals who were charged but never convicted of a criminal offense also are eligible for expungement, regardless of the nature of the crime. An individual may petition for the sealing of the criminal records relating to his or her arrest and charge if all proceedings against him or her were resolved in his or her favor, except in cases of not guilty by reason of mental illness.

The Effect of Expungement

After the court enters an order of expungement, the criminal record is sealed, and the existence of the record may not be revealed. The records are not destroyed and may be accessed in limited circumstances by law enforcement agencies.

The individual does not have to acknowledge the arrest or any other part of the record in response to any inquiry made for any purpose.

Expungement for Juveniles

Chapter 15 of the Minnesota Statutes, entitled "Delinquency," provides individuals with the opportunity to expunge juvenile records. The statutes are vague, and do not provide a method for petitioning the court for expungement. The statutes are summarized below.

> In the case of a juvenile adjudicated delinquent or a juvenile adjudicated as a petty offender, unless the juvenile was transferred to legal custody, the court may expunge the criminal records of the juvenile at any time it feels appropriate.

Other Remedies

Article V, Section 7 of the Minnesota Constitution gives the Governor, with the help of the Board of Pardons, the power to grant pardons for criminal convictions. If the Governor grants a pardon extraordinary, the criminal conviction is set aside and the individual is no longer required to report it except in limited circumstances. The Board receives and reviews applications for eligibility before the Governor makes a decision on an application.

Minnesota Board of Pardons contact information:

(651) 642-0284
Minnesota Board of Pardons
1450 Energy Park Drive, Suite 200
Saint Paul, MN 55108

Conclusion

In Minnesota, expungement is available only in a limited number of circumstances. To obtain an order of expungement, the court must find by clear and convincing evidence that the benefits of expungement outweigh the disadvantages. This type of legal standard is best argued by an experienced attorney.

As we have said multiple times throughout this book "DO NOT TRY THIS AT HOME." There are tons of pitfalls and perils for those trying to obtain an expunction on their own without the help of an attorney. We've said it before and we'll say it now, *do not try a do it yourself expunction.*

The primary problem is "do it yourselfers" can stir up a long dormant and as of yet un-pursued case. In other words, if you go making haphazard inquiries in the wrong case you can arouse prosecutorial interest and fire up an investigation of you and your case/arrest. Thus, use the resource section of our website at www.ultimatesecondchance.com/resources to help find an attorney in your area.

MISSISSIPPI

Introduction

In Mississippi, the statutes allow for the expungement of certain types of criminal convictions. The state also has developed alternative sentencing programs that may provide the opportunity for expungement in a greater number of cases.

The Law in Mississippi

Section 99-19-71 of the Mississippi Code of Criminal Procedure provides for expungement for first-time misdemeanor conviction. The statute is summarized below.

> An individual who was convicted for the first time of a misdemeanor criminal offense, excluding traffic violations, may petition the court for an order expunging the record of the incident.

Section 99-15-59 of the Mississippi Code of Criminal Procedure provides for expungement in cases where charges never were filed or charges were later dropped. The statute is summarized below.

> An individual who was arrested for any misdemeanor but not formally charged or

prosecuted within 12 months from the arrest, or an individual against whom charges are dropped, may petition the court for an order to expunge the record of the arrest.

Section 99-15-26 of the Mississippi Code of Criminal Procedure establishes the option of probation for non-violent offenders. After an individual successfully completes all the conditions of probation, the prosecutor drops all charges and the record may be expunged. The statute is summarized below.

If an individual enters a plea of guilty to any felony or misdemeanor, except for crimes against the person, the court may withhold the sentence pending the successful completion of a probationary program. An individual may qualify for this option only once.

After the individual successfully completes the probationary program, the court will dismiss the cause and close the case. The individual may then petition the court to expunge the record. The court will enter an order for expungement in any case where an arrest was made, the individual arrested was released and the case was dismissed or the charges were dropped or there was no disposition of such case.

Section 9-23-23 of the Mississippi Code of Criminal Procedure establishes another alternative sentencing program similar to probation. If an individual completes all the requirements imposed by the drug court, he or she may be eligible to have his or her record expunged. The statute is summarized below.

> If an individual completes all the requirements imposed by the drug court, the charges will be dismissed. If the individual originally pled guilty at the time of sentencing, the successful completion of the drug court requirements will result in the record being expunged.

Eligibility

Expungement is available for most first-time misdemeanor convictions and it also may be available after the successful completion of certain alternative sentencing programs established by the state. The statutes do, however, exempt certain types of criminal convictions from the possibility of expungement. Except for juvenile criminal history information that has been sealed by order of the court, sex offenses may not be expunged or sealed. The expungement provisions of the statutes specifically exclude traffic violations, and therefore DUI convictions may not be expunged.

Effect of Expungement

If the court enters an expungement, all references to

the individual are erased or blacked out of the public record. A nonpublic record of the offense is retained by the court and by the Mississippi Criminal Information Center and may be used in later proceedings to determine first-time offender status. The individual is restored to the status occupied before the arrest, and does not have to acknowledge the arrest or conviction in response to any inquiry for any purpose.

Expungement for Juveniles

Sections 43-21-261 through 43-21-465 of the Mississippi Code outline the confidentiality requirements of Mississippi Youth Court records. Mississippi, like most other states, grants more protection to juvenile offenders and strictly limits access to most juvenile records. The statutes are summarized below.

Juvenile records may be disclosed only to the staff of the youth court or by court order to certain limited groups of individuals and government agencies.

The youth court may order the sealing of records involving juveniles in the following circumstances:

1. The juvenile has reached the age of 20;

2. The youth court dismissed the cause; or

3. The youth court set aside adjudication in the cause.

The youth court, at its own discretion, may order the sealing or unsealing of the juvenile records at any time. The youth court also may order the destruction of any records involving juveniles except medical or mental health examinations.

Other Remedies

Though short of the relief of expungement, Section 45-27-11 of the Mississippi Code allows individuals to review their criminal records and challenge any possible inaccuracies. The statute is summarized below.

The Mississippi Criminal Information Center must allow an individual to inspect his or her criminal record information upon request. The individual must submit a set of fingerprints and sign a written authorization in order to gain access to his or her records. If the individual believes his or her criminal record information is inaccurate or incomplete, he or she can request the original agency with control over the records to change or delete them. If the agency declines to modify the records, the individual may appeal to the appropriate court within 30 days of the decision by the agency. The court will conduct a hearing and may order the relief required by law.

Article 5, Section 124 of the Mississippi Constitution gives the Governor the power to grant pardons for criminal convictions. The Mississippi Parole Board investigates pardon applications made to the Governor. An individual is required to wait seven years after the completion of his or her sentence before applying for a pardon, and the individual also must post notice in the newspaper of the county in which he or she was convicted describing the reasons the pardon should be granted 30 days before making an application.

Mississippi Parole Board contact information:

(601) 354-7716
Mississippi Parole Board
201 W. Capitol Street, Suite 800
Jackson, MS 39201

Conclusion

In Mississippi, the statutes allow for the expungement of certain, limited types of criminal convictions. The statutes are vague regarding the procedure that an individual must follow and the steps the court will take when determining whether to grant a request for impingement. Due to the vague statutes and the complications that may arise in the process, it is best to get the help of an experienced attorney.

As we have said multiple times throughout this book

"DO NOT TRY THIS AT HOME." There are tons of pitfalls and perils for those trying to obtain an expunction on their own without the help of an attorney. We've said it before and we'll say it now, ***do not try a do it yourself expunction.***

The primary problem is "do it yourselfers" can stir up a long dormant and as of yet un-pursued case. In other words, if you go making haphazard inquiries in the wrong case you can arouse prosecutorial interest and fire up an investigation of you and your case/arrest. Thus, use the resource section of our website at www.ultimatesecondchance.com/resources to help find an attorney in your area.

MISSOURI

Introduction

In Missouri, expungement generally is reserved for individuals who were arrested due to false information. Missouri also provides for the expungement of certain alcohol-related driving offenses.

The Law in Missouri

Section 610.122 of the Missouri Statutes outlines the circumstances in which a criminal record may be expunged. Expungement under this statute is allowed only if the individual seeking expungement was arrested due to false information. The statute is summarized below.

> An individual's arrest record may be expunged if the court determines the individual was arrested due to false information and the following conditions exist:
>
> 1. No probable cause to believe the individual committed the offense existed;
>
> 2. No charges were filed as a result of the arrest;
>
> 3. The individual has no prior or subsequent misdemeanor or felony convictions;

4. The individual did not receive a suspended imposition of sentence for the offense; and

5. No civil action is pending relating to the incident.

Section 610.123 of the Missouri Statutes establishes the procedure an individual seeking expungement under the previous section must follow. The petition must include all of the required information or it will be dismissed. The statute is summarized below.

> An individual seeking to expunge his or her criminal record can file a petition for expungement in the civil division of the court. The petition that must be filed can be found in Rule 155 of the Missouri Rules, entitled "Expungement of Arrest Records." The petition must include the following information:
>
> 1. The individual's full name, sex, race, date of birth, driver's license number, Social Security number, and address;
>
> 2. The offense for which the individual was charged;
>
> 3. The date the individual was arrested;
>
> 4. The name of the county where the individual was arrested;

5. The name of the arresting agency;

6. The case number and court; and

7. The individual's fingerprints on a standard fingerprint card.

The petition must name all law enforcement agencies, courts, prosecuting attorneys, and central state depositories of criminal records as defendants.

The court will conduct a hearing on the matter, and if the court finds that the individual is entitled to expungement, it will enter an order accordingly.

Section 302.545 of the Missouri Statutes provides that first-time offenders under the age of 21 may have the record of a driver's license suspension or revocation for driving under the influence expunged. Only the records concerning the administrative action (the suspension or revocation) are expunged, and not the record of the underlying offense. The statute is summarized below.

If an individual under the age of 21 has his or her driver's license suspended or revoked due to a first-time offense for driving with two-hundredths of one percent of blood alcohol content (not enough for a DWI) the record of the suspension or revocation will be expunged two years after the date of the suspension or when the individual reaches the age of 21, whichever occurs later. Individuals who have their licenses revoked a second time or who are convicted for a DWI or driving with excessive blood alcohol content are not eligible for expungement.

Section 577.054 of the Missouri Statutes takes the previous section one step further. It allows for the one-time expungement of an alcohol-related misdemeanor driving offense. The statute is summarized below.

An individual who was convicted of an alcohol-related, misdemeanor driving offense may petition the court to expunge the record of the offense after ten years have passed since the date of conviction, and the individual has not been convicted of any other alcohol-related driving offenses.

The court will conduct a hearing and if it determines the individual is eligible for expungement, the court will enter an order of expungement. An individual is eligible for expungement of an alcohol-related misdemeanor driving offense only once.

Eligibility

In Missouri, the statutes allow expungement in certain, limited situations. To expunge an arrest record for most offenses, the individual must have been arrested due to false information. In other words, the individual must be factually innocent. One statute, however, allows for the expungement of alcohol-related misdemeanor driving offenses. This type of expungement is available to an individual only once.

Effect of Expungement

After the court enters an order for expungement, the records become confidential and may be accessed only by the parties or by court order. If expungement occurs under Section 610.123 of the Missouri Statutes, all records are destroyed. The effect of an order granting expungement is to restore the individual to the status he or she occupied before the arrest, as if it never took place. An individual need not acknowledge the arrest or conviction in response to any inquiry for any purpose.

Expungement for Juveniles

Missouri, like most states, provides greater confidentiality to the records of a juvenile offender. Section 211.321 of the Missouri Statutes provides for limited access to juvenile court records as well as the possibility of the destruction and sealing of records. The statute is summarized below.

Juvenile court records are confidential and are not open to inspection, except by court order, unless the juvenile was charged with a crime that would be a Class A felony if committed by an adult, such as capital murder, first degree murder, or second degree murder.

The court may, upon its own motion or at the request of the juvenile, enter an order to destroy all juvenile records and seal the official court file, at any time after the juvenile reaches the age of 17.

Other Remedies

Article IV, Section 7 of the Missouri Constitution gives the Governor the power to grant pardons for criminal convictions. The Missouri Board of Probation and Parole reviews all applications for pardon. The individual must wait three years after the completion of his or her sentence to be eligible to apply for a pardon. A pardon does not expunge a criminal record.

Missouri Board of Probation and Parole contact information:

> (573) 751-8488
> Missouri Board of Probation and Parole
> 1511 Christy Drive
> Jefferson City, MO 65101

Conclusion

Missouri allows for expungement only in limited circumstances. The process for applying for and obtaining an order from the court granting expungement is complicated and should not be attempted without the help of an experienced attorney.

As we have said multiple times throughout this book "DO NOT TRY THIS AT HOME." There are tons of pitfalls and perils for those trying to obtain an expungement on their own without the help of an attorney. We've said it before and we'll say it now, *do not try a do it yourself expungement.*

The primary problem is "do it yourselfers" can stir up a long dormant and as of yet un-pursued case. In other words, if you go making haphazard inquiries in the wrong case you can arouse prosecutorial interest and fire up an investigation of you and your case/arrest. Thus, use the resource section of our website at www.ultimatesecondchance.com/resources to help find an attorney in your area.

MONTANA

Introduction

Montana is one of the few states that does not allow for the expungement of criminal records. The Montana code mentions expungement only a few times. Montana courts may order expungement only where a conviction for a sexual or violent offense has been finally reversed. In other cases, it may be possible to request a criminal record be classified as confidential, thereby limiting access to the information.

The Law in Montana

Section 46-23-510 of the Montana Code is the only Montana statute that allows for expungement. This statute allows for the expungement of a record of a conviction for a sexual or violent offense, but only after the conviction has been finally reversed. This type of expungement is automatic. The statute is summarized below.

After the final reversal of a conviction for a sexual or violent offense, the court must order the expungement of any records kept by the court or law enforcement agency.

Section 46-18-204 of the Montana Code provides that if an individual is granted deferred imposition of a sentence, after the time of deferment has elapsed, the individual may request the court to dismiss the charges. If the charges are dismissed, the record is not expunged, but the information contained in the record becomes confidential criminal justice information and may be accessed only by certain, limited government agencies. The statute is summarized below.

> If the court defers the imposition of a sentence for a certain period of time, after the time period has elapsed, the court may allow the individual to withdraw his or her guilty plea or strike the guilty verdict from the record and dismiss the charges against the individual.

> A copy of the dismissal must be sent to the prosecutor and the department of justice. After the charges have been dismissed, all records relating to the charges become confidential criminal justice information and may be accessed only by a court order.

Eligibility

Montana generally does not allow for the expungement of criminal convictions. Individuals who were granted deferred imposition of a sentence may find relief from their criminal records by requesting that the charges be dismissed and the record classified as confidential criminal justice information.

Effect of Confidential Classification

The dissemination of confidential criminal justice information is restricted to criminal justice agencies and those authorized to receive it by a court order.

Sealing of Records for Juveniles

Montana, like many other states, provides greater protection and confidentiality to juvenile criminal records. Section 41-5-216 of the Montana Code provides for the sealing of youth court records once the juvenile reaches the age of 18. The statute is summarized below.

> Youth court records, law enforcement records, and department records must be physically sealed on the juvenile's 18th birthday. The records may be destroyed ten years after the date the records were sealed. Medical records, fingerprints, DNA records, photographs, youth traffic records, and records in cases where the juvenile failed to meet all the court's sentencing requirements may not be sealed. After the records have been sealed, they may be accessed only by certain law enforcement agencies or by court order.

Other Remedies

Article VI, Section 12 of the Montana Constitution gives the Governor the power to grant pardons for criminal convictions. The Montana Board of Pardons and Parole receives and investigates pardon applications. The Board forwards only positive recommendations on to the Governor for consideration.

Montana Board of Pardons and Parole contact information:

> (406) 846-1404
> Montana Board of Pardons and Parole
> 300 Maryland Ave.
> Deer Lodge, MT 59722

Conclusion

Although the availability of expungement is practically non-existent in the State of Montana, it may be possible to ensure the confidentiality of a criminal record. Only individuals granted deferred imposition of sentence are eligible to receive this confidentiality. The help of an experienced attorney is critical to gaining this opportunity.

As we have said multiple times throughout this book "DO NOT TRY THIS AT HOME." There are tons of pitfalls and perils for those trying to obtain relief from a criminal record on their own without the help of an attorney. We've said it before and we'll say it now, *do not try a do it yourself method*.

The primary problem is "do it yourselfers" can stir up a long dormant and as of yet un-pursued case. In other words, if you go making haphazard inquiries in the wrong case you can arouse prosecutorial interest

and fire up an investigation of you and your case/arrest. Thus, use the resource section of our website at www.ultimatesecondchance.com/resources to help find an attorney in your area.

NEBRASKA

Introduction

The Nebraska statutes provide for both expungement and set-aside. The statutes are not clear as to the differing effects of each type of relief. What are clear, however, are strict requirements limiting the types of offenses that may be expunged and set aside.

The Law in Nebraska

Section 29-3523 of the Nebraska Code of Criminal Procedure outlines the circumstances in which an individual may petition for an expungement and the steps an individual must take to obtain that relief. The statute is summarized below.

> If an individual was arrested but not prosecuted, the record of his or her arrest becomes confidential and may only be accessed by criminal justice agencies, unless one of the following situations applies:
>
> 1. The individual currently is awaiting prosecution or is in custody as the result of a separate arrest;
>
> 2. The individual currently is a candidate

for public office or currently holds public office;

3. The individual made a notarized request for the release of the record; or

4. The individual is kept unidentified and the information is used for statistical purposes only.

An individual who was arrested due to a mistake may file a petition with the court for an order expunging the related criminal record. The individual must file the petition in the district court of the county in which he or she was arrested. A copy of the petition must be sent to the county attorney who is to be named in the petition as the respondent.

If the court finds by clear and convincing evidence that the arrest was due to a mistake, the court will enter an order expunging the record.

Section 29-4010 of the Nebraska Code of Criminal Procedure provides that registered sex offenders may petition the court to expunge their information from the sex offender database once their duty to register has expired. The statute is summarized below.

An individual who is required to register under the Sex Offender Registration Act may petition the court for an order to expunge the information unless the individual is required to register for his or her lifetime.

The petition must be filed in the district court of the county where the individual was convicted. A copy of the petition must be sent to the county attorney who is to be named in the petition as the respondent.

If the court finds by clear and convincing evidence that the individual's duty to register has expired, no criminal charges are pending against him or her, and there is not a substantial risk that the individual will repeat the offense, the court will grant an order expunging the record.

The Child Protection Act and the Adult Protective Services Act of the Nebraska Code of Crimes and Punishments allows an individual to request the Department of Health and Human Services to expunge investigative records concerning the individual's possible abuse or neglect of a child or vulnerable adult. The statutes are summarized below.

An individual who was the subject of an investigation by the Department of Health and Human Services, for the abuse or neglect of a child or vulnerable adult, may request that the Department expunge the information from the respective registries. If the Department refuses to expunge the information, the individual has the right to a hearing with the Department to determine whether the record should be expunged on the ground that it is inaccurate. At the end of the hearing, the decision will be made in writing and will state the reasons for the determination. The decision may be appealed.

The Department may expunge a record from the Adult Protective Services Registry or the central register of child protection cases concerning abuse or neglect without being requested at any time it is appropriate.

Section 60-6,211.06 of the Nebraska Motor Vehicle Code outlines the ability to expunge a traffic infraction received by an individual under the age of 21 for operating a motor vehicle under the influence of alcohol. The statute is summarized below.

If an individual under the age of 21 has his or her driver's license impounded for driving with two hundredths of a gram or more by weight blood alcohol content, the infraction will become part of the individual's record for 90 days. After 90 days, the Department of Motor Vehicles will expunge the violation from the individual's record. If the individual refuses to submit to a blood alcohol test, the violation will become part of the individual's record for 120 days. After 120 days the department will expunge the record.

In Nebraska, individuals with criminal convictions, although ineligible for expungement, may petition the court to set aside a criminal conviction. Many other states define set-aside as expungement. Section 29-2264 of the Nebraska Code of Criminal Procedure provides that individuals placed on probation for misdemeanor and felony offenses may petition the court to set aside their conviction after they successfully complete the terms of their probation. The statute is summarized below.

> If an individual is placed on probation for a misdemeanor or felony and successfully completes the conditions of probation ordered by the court, the sentencing court will issue an order releasing the individual from probation. After release from probation, the individual may petition the sentencing court to set aside the conviction.

> When determining whether to set aside a conviction, the court will consider the behavior of the individual after sentencing, the likelihood that the individual will continue to engage in criminal activity, and any other relevant information.

> If the court determines that the order granting a set-aside is in the best interests of the individual and the public, the court will enter an order setting aside the conviction. An order

setting aside the conviction nullifies the conviction and removes all civil disabilities imposed due to the conviction. The conviction, however, may be used as evidence in subsequent prosecutions.

Eligibility

In Nebraska, in order to be eligible to receive expungement of a criminal record, an individual must have been arrested but not actually charged of an offense for at least a year after he or she was arrested. An individual with an actual conviction, misdemeanor or felony, may be eligible to have his or her conviction set aside if he or she successfully completes court-ordered probation. The statutes do not clearly distinguish expungement and set-aside, though convictions that have been set aside may be used in subsequent prosecutions.

Effect of Expungement

Nebraska provides for both expungement and set-aside. When a criminal record is expunged, it is erased in its entirety. If a criminal record is set aside, the information is not actually erased. Instead, set-aside convictions may be used in subsequent prosecutions.

Set-Aside for Juveniles

Section 43-2,105 of the Nebraska Juvenile Code provides for the set-aside of juvenile adjudications. Juvenile records are confidential and subject to limited access. The statute is summarized below.

> If the court issues an order setting aside a juvenile adjudication, the court also must order that all the records be sealed. Sealed juvenile records are not available to the public except by court order.

Other Remedies

Article IV, Section 13 of the Nebraska Constitution creates the Board of Pardons and gives the Governor the power to grant pardons for criminal convictions. The Nebraska Board of Pardons accepts and reviews pardon applications. The Board may decide to conduct a hearing on the application before making a decision. Usually an individual must wait ten years from the completion of a felony sentence and three years from the completion of a misdemeanor sentence before becoming eligible to apply for a pardon.

Nebraska Board of Pardons contact information:

> (402) 479-5726
> Nebraska Board of Pardons
> P.O. Box 94754
> Lincoln, NE 68509

Conclusion

Nebraska provides for both expungement and set-aside. The statutes are not clear as to the different effects of each type of relief. Regardless of the type of relief for which an individual may be eligible, the process can be extremely complex and should not be attempted without the help of an experienced attorney.

As we have said multiple times throughout this book "DO NOT TRY THIS AT HOME." There are tons of pitfalls and perils for those trying to obtain an expungement on their own without the help of an attorney. We've said it before and we'll say it now, *do not try a do it yourself expungement.*

The primary problem is "do it yourselfers" can stir up a long dormant and as of yet un-pursued case. In other words, if you go making haphazard inquiries in the wrong case you can arouse prosecutorial interest and fire up an investigation of you and your case/arrest. Thus, use the resource section of our website at www.ultimatesecondchance.com/resources to help find an attorney in your area.

NEVADA

Introduction

In Nevada, the statutes provide numerous opportunities for an individual to obtain relief from a criminal record in the form of an order to seal the record. Criminal convictions of varying severity may be order sealed under certain circumstances. In many cases, the individual may have to wait a certain period of time before becoming eligible to petition for an order to seal his or her record.

The Law in Nevada

Section 179.245 of the Nevada Statutes allows for the sealing of records for most types of criminal convictions. Before an individual is eligible to petition for the sealing of his or her criminal record he or she must wait a certain period of time depending on the nature of the crime. The statute is summarized below.

> An individual with a criminal conviction may petition the court in which he or she was convicted for the sealing of his criminal record after a specific statutory waiting period. The length of time an individual must wait before becoming eligible to petition the court for a sealing of his or her record depends on the

nature and severity of the crime for which he or she was convicted.

The petition must contain the records of the individual's criminal history from The Central Repository for Nevada Records of Criminal History and the arresting law enforcement agency. The petition must also list any other agency that may possess a copy of the records and include information that accurately identifies the records to be sealed.

The court will notify the arresting law enforcement agency and the prosecuting attorney upon receiving the petition and conduct a hearing on the matter. The prosecuting attorney and any other individuals with relevant information may testify at a hearing on the petition. If the court determines at the hearing that the individual has not been charged with another crime since the date he or she completed his or her sentence and the date of the petition, the court can order all of the records sealed.

Section 179.255 of the Nevada Statutes allows for the sealing of records for individuals who were arrested but never convicted of a criminal offense. The statute is similar to the sealing statute for criminal convictions except that there is no required waiting period.

If an individual was arrested for a criminal offense but was later acquitted or the charges were dismissed, he or she may petition the court for the sealing of the records at any time after the date of dismissal or acquittal.

The petition must contain the records of the individual's criminal history from The Central Repository for Nevada Records of Criminal History and the arresting law enforcement agency. The petition must also list any other agency that may possess a copy of the records and include information that accurately identifies the records to be sealed.

The court will notify the arresting law enforcement agency and the prosecuting attorney upon receiving the petition and conduct a hearing on the matter. The prosecuting attorney and any other individuals with relevant information may testify at a hearing on the petition. If the court determines at the hearing that the individual was in fact acquitted or that all the charges were dismissed against him or her, the court will order all of the records sealed.

Section 176A.265 of the Nevada Statutes, entitled "Sealing of Records after Discharge," allows for the sealing of records for individuals who successfully complete all the terms and conditions of probation imposed upon them by the court. The statute is summarized below.

> Three years after an individual successfully completes and is discharged from probation, the court will order all of the records sealed. The court will not conduct a hearing on the matter unless requested by the division of parole and probation.

Section 179.259 of the Nevada Statutes allows for the sealing of records for individuals who complete a program for reentry. The statute is summarized below.

> Five years after an eligible individual completes a program for reentry, the court may seal all the records relating to the case. The court will not conduct a hearing on the matter unless requested by the division of parole and probation.

> Records sealed pursuant to this statute may be accessed by a professional licensing board for the purpose of determining eligibility for a license or disciplinary action.

Section 453.3365 of the Nevada Code is part of the Nevada Controlled Substances Act. The statute provides for the sealing of criminal records for people convicted of possession of controlled substances *not for the purpose of sale*. The statute is summarized below.

If an individual was convicted of unlawful possession of a controlled substance not for purposes of sale, the court may seal all the records relating to the offense three years after the conviction. Before the court may seal the records, the individual must have fulfilled the terms and conditions of probation and the court must be satisfied that the individual is rehabilitated.

Records sealed pursuant to this statute may be accessed by a professional licensing board for the purpose of determining eligibility for a license or disciplinary action.

Eligibility

In the event an individual has a criminal conviction, there are statutory waiting periods that must pass before the individual becomes eligible to petition the court for the sealing of the criminal records. An individual may petition the court for the sealing of a criminal record relating to a Category A or B felony conviction 15 years after the completion of his or her sentence. For Category C and D felonies, an individual must wait 12 years after the completion of his or her sentence, and for a Category E felony conviction, or any gross or violent misdemeanor, an individual must wait until seven years pass after the completion of his or her sentence before he or she is eligible to petition the court for a sealing of the criminal record. Any other misdemeanor convictions require a waiting period of two years from the date the individual completed his or her sentence before the individual becomes eligible to petition the court to seal his or her record. Records relating to a conviction for a crime against a child or a sexual offense may never be sealed.

Effect of Sealing Records

After the court grants an order to seal an individual's criminal record, the proceedings are deemed never to have occurred, and the individual does not have to acknowledge the record in response to any inquiry relating to an application for employment. The individual's rights to vote, hold office, and serve on a jury are immediately restored.

The Sealing of Records for Juveniles

Chapter 62H of the Nevada Statutes deals with juvenile justice. In Nevada, like many other states, the statutes provide greater relief to juvenile offenders. The chapter outlines the eligibility requirements and procedures for obtaining an order sealing juvenile criminal records. The statutes are summarized below.

> When a juvenile is less than 21 years of age, the juvenile or his or her probation officer may petition the juvenile court for an order sealing all records relating to the juvenile. The petition may not be filed until three years have passed since the juvenile was last adjudicated delinquent, or referred to the juvenile court, whichever occurs later.

The juvenile court will notify the district attorney and the probation officer upon receiving the petition and conduct a hearing on the matter. The district attorney and any individuals with relevant information may testify at the hearing. If the court determines at the hearing that the juvenile has not been convicted of a felony or a misdemeanor involving moral turpitude since the date of filing of the petition, and that the juvenile has been rehabilitated, the court will grant an order to seal the record.

When a juvenile reaches the age of 21, all his or her juvenile records are automatically sealed.

If a juvenile was convicted of an unlawful act in a special category, such as a sexual assault, battery with the intent to commit sexual assault, lewdness with a child, or an unlawful act which would have been a felony if committed by an adult, and if the record was not sealed prior to the juvenile reaching the age of 21, the record may not be sealed until the juvenile reaches the age of 30.

Lesser Remedies

Article V, Section 14 of the Nevada Constitution gives the Governor the power to grant pardons for criminal convictions. After completing his or her sentence, an individual may submit an application for pardon to the

Executive Secretary of the Pardons Board. A pardon does not erase the conviction from the individual's criminal record, and generally the board will only accept applications from individuals after a significant amount of time has passed since the completion of their sentence.

Nevada Board of Pardons contact information:

(775) 687-8278
Board of Pardons Commissioners
1445 Old Hot Springs Rd. #108B
Carson City, NV 89711

Conclusion

In Nevada, the statutes provide the relief in the form of sealing of criminal records for several types of criminal convictions. Despite the relatively unrestricted availability of obtaining an order granting a sealing of records, the process of petitioning for such an order is complex and time consuming. It is best to enlist the help of an experienced attorney.

As we have said multiple times throughout this book "DO NOT TRY THIS AT HOME." There are tons of pitfalls and perils for those trying to obtain an order sealing records on their own without the help of an attorney. We've said it before and we'll say it now, *do not try to do it yourself.*

The primary problem is "do it yourselfers" can stir up a long dormant and as of yet un-pursued case. In other words, if you go making haphazard inquiries in the wrong case you can arouse prosecutorial interest and fire up an investigation of you and your case/arrest. Thus, use the resource section of our website at www.ultimatesecondchance.com/resources to help find an attorney in your area.

NEW HAMPSHIRE

Introduction

In New Hampshire, the statutes provide for relief from the effects of a criminal record in the form of annulment. After a statutorily prescribed time period, an individual may petition the court to annul his or her criminal record. An annulment effectively seals the criminal history information.

The Law in New Hampshire

Section 651:5 of the New Hampshire Criminal Code, entitled "Annulment of Criminal Records," provides that individuals with a criminal record, including criminal convictions, may petition the sentencing court to annul the records relating to the offense. The statute is summarized below.

An individual who was convicted of a criminal offense may petition the sentencing court for an annulment of his or her criminal record. Upon receiving the petition, the Department of Corrections will investigate the individual's criminal record and report the findings to the court. The Department of Corrections may charge the individual a fee of $100 to cover the cost of the investigation. If the court determines the individual is eligible for annulment based on the Department's investigation, the court will conduct a hearing on the matter. The court will notify the prosecuting attorney of the petition and will allow him or her to testify at the hearing. If the individual does not meet the eligibility requirements for annulment, the court will dismiss the petition without a hearing. If the court conducts a hearing and determines the annulment will assist the individual's rehabilitation and be consistent with the public welfare, the court will annul the record.

Section 169-C:35 of the New Hampshire Statutes, entitled "Central Registry," establish a state registry for reports of child abuse and neglect, and provides for methods to expunge records from the registry. The statute is summarized below.

Substantiated reports of child abuse and neglect must be maintained in the registry for a period of seven years. An individual has the right to petition the district court to expunge his or her information from the registry before the seven years have expired. The individual must wait one year from the date his or her name and information was placed in the registry before the individual can file a petition in the district court requesting expungement. The court will require the Department of Health and Human Services to file a report on the individual. After receiving the report, the court can act on the petition without conducting a hearing. If the court determines that the individual is not a current threat to the safety of children, the court will expunge the information from the registry.

Eligibility

In New Hampshire, if an individual was arrested but was either acquitted, not prosecuted, or whose case was dismissed, may petition the court for annulment of the record at any time. An individual who was convicted of a criminal offense may petition the court for annulment of the record when the individual has completed all the terms and conditions of the sentence and has not been convicted of another offense for a certain period of time. The time period an individual must wait before becoming eligible to petition for annulment depends on the nature of the underlying offense. If an individual was convicted of a violation, he or she must not be convicted of another offense for one year before being eligible to petition for annulment. Individuals convicted of Class B and A misdemeanors must wait a period of three years without being convicted of another offense before becoming eligible to petition for annulment.

Individuals convicted of a Class B felony must wait a period of five years, and individuals convicted of a Class A felony, sexual assault, or felony indecent exposure must wait a period of ten years. Individuals convicted of a violent crime, obstruction of justice, or any offense for which the individual was sentenced to an extended term of imprisonment may not petition for annulment. Individuals with more than one criminal conviction may not petition for annulment if any part of their record is barred from annulment.

Effect of Annulment

After receiving an order of annulment, the individual whose record was annulled is treated as if he or she has never been arrested or convicted. The individual need not acknowledge the conviction in response to any inquiry for any purpose. Convictions that have been annulled may be considered, however, in another prosecution and can be counted toward habitual offender status.

Juvenile Records

Section 169-B:35 of the New Hampshire Statutes provide that juvenile records related to delinquency are confidential and may be accessed only by a limited number of individuals. The statute is summarized below.

All juvenile records related to delinquency are confidential. Juvenile court records are to be kept in files separate from all other court records, and the records are not available for public inspection. The records may be inspected, however, by law enforcement personnel or by court order. Once a juvenile reaches the age of 21, all the records are to be closed and placed in an inactive file.

Other Remedies

Part 2, Article 52 of the New Hampshire Constitution

gives the Governor the power to grant pardons for criminal convictions. The Executive Council reviews pardon applications and recommends the proper course of action for the Governor. The Governor will not issue a pardon unless majority of the Executive Council votes in favor of a pardon. A pardon will not erase a criminal conviction. Pardon applications must be submitted to the Office of the Attorney General.

New Hampshire Office of Attorney General contact information:

(603) 271-3658
Office of the Attorney General
State of New Hampshire
33 Capitol Street
Concord, NH 03301

Conclusion

In New Hampshire, the statutes provide for relief from a criminal record in the form of annulment. Most types of convictions are eligible for annulment after a certain time has passed since the conviction. The process of requesting and obtaining relief, however, is complex and should not be attempted without the help of an experienced attorney.

As we have said multiple times throughout this book "DO NOT TRY THIS AT HOME." There are tons of pitfalls and perils for those trying to obtain an annulment on their own without the help of an attorney. We've said it before and we'll say it now, do not try a do it yourself annulment.

The primary problem is "do it yourselfers" can stir up a long dormant and as of yet un-pursued case. In other words, if you go making haphazard inquiries in the wrong case you can arouse prosecutorial interest and fire up an investigation of you and your case/arrest. Thus, use the resource section of our website at www.ultimatesecondchance.com/resources to help find an attorney in your area.

NEW JERSEY

Introduction

In New Jersey, the statutes provide for the expungement of a wide variety of criminal records, including criminal convictions. The New Jersey Code of Criminal Justice dedicates an entire chapter to the requirements and procedures for obtaining the expungement of a criminal record.

The Law in New Jersey

Chapter 52 of the New Jersey Code of Criminal Justice, entitled "Expungement of Records," contains a variety of statutes outlining the eligibility requirements and effect of expungement as well as the procedure to follow when petitioning the court for an order expunging criminal records. The statutes are summarized below.

> If an individual has only one conviction and has not been adjudged a disorderly person on more than two occasions, he or she may petition the Superior Court to expunge all records of the conviction ten years after the completion of his or her sentence. An individual with a conviction for a disorderly person offense may petition the court for expungement five years after the completion of

his or her sentence, and an individual who has been found guilty of violating a municipal ordinance may petition the court for an expungement two years after the completion of the sentence. An individual convicted for the possession or use of a controlled dangerous substance who was 21 years old or younger at the time of the offense may petition the court to expunge the record one year after the completion of the sentence. In all cases, the individual must not have any prior or subsequent criminal convictions.

If an individual was arrested for a criminal offense but the proceedings were dismissed, or the individual was acquitted or discharged without a conviction, he or she may petition the court to expunge the record at any time after the disposition of proceedings. An individual who had the charges against him or her dismissed pursuant to probation or a similar supervisory program may petition the court to expunge the record six months after the dismissal. An individual who had the charges against him or her dismissed due to a determination of insanity may not petition the court for expungement.

A petition for expungement filed with the court must be verified and include the following information:

1. The individual's date of birth;

2. The date the individual was arrested;

3. The statute or offense for which the individual was charged or convicted;

4. The original indictment, summons, or complaint number;

5. The date of conviction or disposition of the matter; and

6. The court's disposition and the punishment imposed.

The petition also must be accompanied by a statement that no criminal charges are pending against the individual and that the individual has not been granted an expungement previously. A $30 fee must be paid to the State Treasurer upon submission of the petition.

After receiving a petition for expungement, the court will schedule a hearing on the matter. A copy of the petition must be sent to the Superintendent of State Police, the Attorney General, the County Prosecutor, and the Chief of Police. If no one in that group objects to the expungement, the court may grant expungement without a hearing. If, at a hearing, the court determines the desirability of the individual to be freed from the disabilities of the conviction outweighs the need for the availability of the records, the court will enter an order for expungement.

Eligibility

In New Jersey, the statutes allow for expungement of a wide variety of criminal convictions. The nature of the conviction determines length of time an individual must wait before becoming eligible to petition the court for expungement. The statutes do, however, exempt records of certain criminal convictions from the possibility of expungement. Criminal records regarding convictions for murder, manslaughter, treason, anarchy, kidnapping, rape, forcible sodomy, arson, perjury, false swearing, robbery, embracery, and conspiracy, may not be expunged. Records regarding a conviction for any crime committed by an individual holding public office may not be expunged if the crime involved the public office. Convictions for the sale or distribution of a controlled dangerous substance or possession with the intent to sell a controlled dangerous substance may not be expunged unless the crime relates to marijuana, where the quantity was 25 grams or less, or hashish, where the quantity was five grams or less.
Convictions for motor vehicle offenses may not be expunged.

Effect of Expungement

In New Jersey, expungement means the extraction

and isolation of all records relating to a criminal offense. After an order of expungement is entered, the arrest and conviction are deemed never to have occurred, and the individual need not acknowledge the existence of the record in response to a direct question. The records may be accessed, however, by law enforcement agencies and the judicial branch of the government for employment purposes and in the event of subsequent criminal proceedings, or by a court order.

Expungement for Juveniles

Section 2A:4A-62 of the New Jersey Statutes, entitled "Sealing of Records," provides for the confidentiality of all juvenile legal records. The expungement of juvenile records is governed by Chapter 52 of the New Jersey Code of Criminal Justice and the statutes providing for the expungement of adult criminal records. The statutes are summarized below.

At the request of the juvenile or on the court's own motion, the court may order the nondisclosure of social, medical, psychological, and legal records of the juvenile if two years have passed since the juvenile was discharged from custody of supervision and the juvenile has not been convicted of a crime or adjudicated delinquent in that time. The two-year waiting period may be waived for juveniles enlisting in any branch of the United States Armed Forces.

Notice of the motion to seal the records must be sent to the Attorney General, the county prosecutor, the authority granting final discharge, and the law enforcement agency with custody of the records.

Upon the entry of an order sealing the records, the juvenile may reply that no record exists in response to any direct inquiry.

A juvenile who has been adjudicated delinquent may have his or her entire record expunged if five or more years have passed since the completion of the sentence and he or she has not been convicted of another crime in that time. The expungement of juvenile records is governed by the statutes for adult expungement.

Other Remedies

Article V, Section 2 of the New Jersey Constitution gives the Governor the power to grant pardons for criminal convictions. The Governor refers applications to the New Jersey Parole Board for investigation and recommendation, but the Governor has the final say. A pardon can allow for the expungement of an offense that is ineligible for expungement according to the Code of Criminal Justice.

New Jersey Office of The Governor contact information:

(609) 292-6000
Office of the Governor
P.O. Box 001
Trenton, NJ 08625

Conclusion

In New Jersey, the statutes provide for expungement for a variety of criminal convictions. The process of obtaining expungement of a criminal record is complex and should not be attempted without the help of an experienced attorney.

As we have said multiple times throughout this book "DO NOT TRY THIS AT HOME." There are tons of pitfalls and perils for those trying to obtain an expungement on their own without the help of an attorney. We've said it before and we'll say it now, *do not try a do it yourself expungement.*

The primary problem is "do it yourselfers" can stir up a long dormant and as of yet un-pursued case. In other words, if you go making haphazard inquiries in the wrong case you can arouse prosecutorial interest and fire up an investigation of you and your case/arrest. Thus, use the resource section of our website at www.ultimatesecondchance.com/resources to help find an attorney in your area.

NEW MEXICO

Introduction

In New Mexico, the statutes do not provide for expungement of any adult conviction information. Expungement still may be available to hide arrest information for which a conviction did not result, and expungement also may be used if an individual is placed on deferred adjudication or a similar diversionary program.

The Law in New Mexico

Section 29-3-8.1 of the New Mexico Statutes, entitled "Petition to Expunge Arrest Information," outlines the circumstances in which an individual may petition the Department of Public Safety for the expungement of arrest information. The language of the statute is rather vague and appears to be severely limited in availability. The statute is summarized below.

> An individual arrested for a misdemeanor or a petty misdemeanor that does not involve a crime of moral turpitude may petition the Department of Public Safety to expunge the information relating to the arrest. If the Department cannot find a final disposition relating to the arrest, the Department must expunge the arrest information.

Section 30-31-28 of the New Mexico Statutes outlines the availability of deferred adjudication for offenses involving the possession of a controlled substance. The statute is unclear as to the effect of dismissal for adult offenders, but it does state that juvenile offenders may petition for expungement of the record. The statute is summarized below.

> If an individual is convicted for the possession of a controlled substance and the individual has never before been convicted of any other offense related to narcotic drugs, marijuana, hallucinogenic or depressant or stimulant substances, the court may defer proceedings against him or her without entering a judgment of guilty and place him or her on probation. If the individual successfully completes the terms and conditions of probation, the court will discharge him or her and will dismiss the proceedings. Once the charges have been dismissed, the individual is deemed never to have been convicted. An individual is eligible for this type of dismissal only once.

> If the individual was a juvenile under the age of 18 at the time of the offense, he or she may apply to the court for an order to expunge the records relating to the offense. The court will conduct a hearing and, if the court determines that the juvenile was dismissed and the proceedings against him or her were

discharged, it will enter an order for expungement.

Eligibility

An individual who was arrested for a misdemeanor or petty misdemeanor not involving moral turpitude may petition for the expungement of the arrest information. Only final dispositions of *nolle prosequi*, dismissal, decision to not file charges, referral to a diversion program, placement on probation, or imposition of a fine may be expunged. Adult convictions may not be expunged or sealed. Certain, special provisions exist for offenses regarding the possession of a controlled substance. An individual placed on probation for the possession of a controlled substance may be eligible for expungement after successfully completing the terms and conditions of probation.

Effect of Expungement

In New Mexico, expungement of an arrest record means the removal of a notation of an arrest on the individual's state or FBI record. Once information is expunged, it is as if the incident never occurred, and the individual need not acknowledge the arrest in response to any inquiry for any purpose. A non-public record of the offense is maintained by the attorney general for possible use in future criminal proceedings.

Expungement for Juveniles

In New Mexico, like many other states, the statutes are more forgiving of juvenile offenders. While adult convictions may not be expunged in New Mexico, most juvenile offense may be expunged. Section 32A-3B-21 of the New Mexico Children's Code, entitled "Expungement of Records," outlines the availability of expungement for juvenile offenses. The statute is summarized below.

> The court, on a motion by the juvenile or on its own motion, may vacate its judgment against the juvenile and order the records of the court and any other agency expunged. An order expunging records will be entered if the court finds that:
>
> 1. Two years have passed since the juvenile was released from legal custody and supervision; and
>
> 2. The juvenile has not been convicted of a felony or misdemeanor involving moral turpitude or found delinquent by a court in that two-year period, and no proceedings against him or her are pending.
>
> Notice of the motion will be given to the children's court attorney, the authority that granted final release from custody or probation, and the law enforcement office with

custody of the records.

After the court enters an order for expungement, it shall be as if the incident never occurred and all records will be deleted. The juvenile need not acknowledge the record in response to any inquiry for any purpose. The records may be used by the court, however, in subsequent delinquency proceedings.

Other Remedies

Section 29-10-8 of the New Mexico Statutes provides for the right of an individual to review his or her arrest information, challenge the accuracy of the records, and request corrections to the records. If the law enforcement agency in charge of the records refuses to make the appropriate corrections, the individual may appeal the decision to the district court.

Article V, Section 6 of the New Mexico Constitution gives the Governor the power to grant pardons for criminal convictions. The Parole Board investigates all pardon applications and forwards recommendations to the Governor. Usually an individual must wait five to ten years after the completion of his or her sentence, depending on the nature of the crime, before becoming eligible to apply for a pardon.

New Mexico Pardons and Paroles contact information:

(505) 476-2265
Pardons/Paroles
Office of the Governor
State Capitol Building
Santa Fe, NM 87501

Conclusion

In New Mexico, the statutes name two types of relief from a criminal record: sealing of records and expungement. The sealing of records is the only relief provided by statute, however, and the circumstances in which an individual may obtain an order granting the sealing of criminal records are limited. In any case, do not attempt to petition for the sealing of a record, or an expungement, without the help of an experienced attorney.

As we have said multiple times throughout this book "DO NOT TRY THIS AT HOME." There are tons of pitfalls and perils for those trying to obtain a sealing of records on their own without the help of an attorney. We've said it before and we'll say it now, *do not try a "do it yourself sealing of records."*

The primary problem is "do it yourselfers" can stir up a long dormant and as of yet un-pursued case. In other words, if you go making haphazard inquiries in the wrong case you can arouse prosecutorial interest and fire up an investigation of you and your case/arrest. Thus, use the resource section of our website at www.ultimatesecondchance.com/resources to help find an attorney in your area.

NEW YORK

Introduction

In New York, the statutes provide that the records of a criminal offense may be sealed if the proceedings in the case were terminated in favor of the individual who is the subject of the records. The New York statutes also mention the availability of expungement. The statutes do not provide for the relief of expungement, rather, it is considered an inherent power of the courts that may be exercised at their discretion.

The Law in New York

Section 160.50 of the New York Code of Criminal Procedure outlines the circumstances in which a court will seal the records relating to a criminal proceeding. The general requirement for sealing is that the proceedings must be terminated in the individual's favor. The statute is summarized below.

> If a criminal proceeding against an individual is terminated in his or her favor, the record of the proceedings must be sealed unless the court or the district attorney demonstrates that the interests of justice require otherwise.

A criminal proceeding against an individual is considered terminated in his or her favor in the following circumstances:

1. The trial or appellate court enters an order dismissing all charges;

2. The court enters an order dismissing all charges pursuant to an adjournment in contemplation of dismissal;

3. The court enters an order terminating the prosecution against the individual;

4. The court enters a verdict of acquittal;

5. The court enters an order setting aside;

6. The court enters an order vacating a conviction;

7. The court enters an order of discharge on a ground that invalidates the conviction;

8. The prosecutor chooses not to prosecute the individual;

9. The arresting police agency chooses not to proceed; or

10. The charges include a violation of an offense involving marijuana where the sole substance involved was marijuana, and three years have passed since the offense occurred.

Eligibility

In New York, to be eligible to petition for the sealing of a criminal record, all charges against the individual must have been resolved in his or her favor. Proceedings can be terminated in an individual's favor in a number of ways. For example, an order granting adjournment in contemplation of dismissal that is eventually dismissed due to the individual's successful completion of all the terms and conditions required by the court will result in the sealing of the record. A court may grant an adjournment in contemplation of dismissal in cases involving misdemeanor offenses, certain marijuana violations, and a few alcohol-related driving offenses for individuals under the age of 21.

Effect of Sealing Records

In New York, if a criminal record is sealed, all photographs and fingerprints of the individual either must be destroyed or returned to the individual. Only the individual who is the subject of the records and a limited number of government and law enforcement agencies may gain access to sealed records. After an individual receives an order granting the sealing of his or her record, he or she is restored to the position he or she maintained prior to the arrest, and it is as if the incident never happened.

Sealing Records for Juveniles

In New York, like many other states, the statutes provide more relief for juvenile offenders. Section 354.1 of the New York Family Court Act outlines the circumstances in which juvenile criminal information will be destroyed. The statute is summarized below.

If a juvenile was adjudicated delinquent for anything other than a felony by the family court, all fingerprints, photographs, and information must be destroyed.

Information regarding felony adjudications involving 11- and 12-year old offenders may only be retained only if the offense is a Class A or Class B felony.

Records concerning juveniles over age 12 with a felony adjudication, and juveniles 11 and 12 years of age with a Class A or Class B felony adjudication must be destroyed at the time the juvenile reaches the age of 21 or has been discharged from custody or supervision for three years, whichever occurs later. The records of juvenile felony adjudications will be destroyed only if no other criminal convictions or criminal proceedings are pending against him or her at the time the record becomes eligible for destruction.

Other Remedies

Article IV, Section 4 of the New York Constitution gives the Governor the power to grant pardons for criminal convictions. The Governor grants pardons only in exceptional and highly meritorious circumstances. Other possible forms of relief include a certificate of relief from disabilities or a certificate of good conduct. Information concerning pardons and certificates may be obtained from the New York State Board of Parole.

New York State Board of Parole contact information:

(518) 485-8953
Director
Executive Clemency Bureau
New York State Division of Parole
97 Central Avenue
Albany, NY 12206

Conclusion

In New York, the statutes name two types of relief from a criminal record: sealing of records and expungement. The sealing of records is the only relief provided by statute, however, and the circumstances in which an individual may obtain an order granting the sealing of criminal records are limited. In any case, do not attempt to petition for the sealing of a record, or an expungement, without the help of an experienced attorney.

As we have said multiple times throughout this book "DO NOT TRY THIS AT HOME." There are tons of pitfalls and perils for those trying to obtain a sealing of records on their own without the help of an attorney. We've said it before and we'll say it now, *do not try a "do it yourself sealing of records."*

The primary problem is "do it yourselfers" can stir up a long dormant and as of yet un-pursued case. In other words, if you go making haphazard inquiries in the wrong case you can arouse prosecutorial interest and fire up an investigation of you and your case/arrest. Thus, use the resource section of our website at www.ultimatesecondchance.com/resources to help find an attorney in your area.

NORTH CAROLINA

Introduction

In North Carolina, the statutes provide for expunction. Expunction may be available for a wide variety of criminal offenses, but it is granted only under the limited circumstance of an actual criminal conviction.

The Law in North Carolina

Article 5 of the North Carolina Criminal Procedure Act, entitled "The Expunction of Records," outlines the different circumstances in which an expunction of a criminal record an individual may obtain. The statutes are summarized below.

> If an individual was charged with a crime as a result of another person using his or her identity and the charge is dismissed, a finding of not guilty is entered, or the conviction is set aside, the individual may petition the court for an order expunging all records relating to the individual's arrest, charge, or trial.

> The court will notify the district attorney and conduct a hearing on the petition. If the court finds the individual's identity was used without permission and the charges were

dismissed, a finding of not guilty was entered, or the conviction was set aside, then the court will order the expunction.

If an individual was charged with a crime, either a misdemeanor or a felony, and the charge was dismissed, or a finding of not guilty or not responsible was entered, the individual may petition the court for an order to expunge all records relating to his or her apprehension or trial.

The court will conduct a hearing on the petition, and if the court determines that the individual has not been convicted previously of a felony or received an order granting expunction, the court will enter the order of expunction.

An individual charged with multiple offenses, whether they arose from the same transaction, may petition for the expunction of all the offenses if the charges were dismissed for each offense, or the individual was found not guilty of each offense, and the separate offenses occurred within the same 12-month period or same term of court.

If an individual was convicted of a crime and received a pardon of innocence, the individual may petition the court for an order to expunge all records relating to the conviction. After the clerk of the court verifies the pardon, the court will issue an order of expunction.

If an individual under the age of 18 who has not been convicted previously of a criminal offense pleads guilty to a misdemeanor, or if an individual under the age of 21 who has not previously been convicted of a criminal offense pleads guilty to a misdemeanor possession of alcohol, he or she may file a petition in the court for expunction of the misdemeanor from his or her criminal record. The petition may not be filed until at least two years have elapsed since the conviction or the completion of probation.

The petition must include the following:

1. An affidavit by the individual that he or she has not been convicted of any other criminal offense since the misdemeanor conviction;

2. Verified affidavits of two people not related to the individual stating that they know the character of the individual and that his or her character is good;

3. A statement that the petition is a motion in the case for which the individual was convicted;

4. Affidavits of the clerk of superior court, chief of police, and sheriff of the county in which the individual was convicted showing that the petitioner has not been convicted of a criminal offense; and

5. An affidavit by the individual that no restitution orders or civil judgments against him or her are outstanding.

The petition must be served upon the district attorney who will have an opportunity to file an objection to the petition.

The court will conduct a hearing on the petition and if the court determines that the individual has been on good behavior, is free of any other convictions, and meets all of the eligibility requirements, the court will order that the individual be restored to the status he or she occupied before the conviction and the misdemeanor be expunged from the records.

For all types of expunction proceedings, with the exception of misdemeanor convictions of individuals under the age of 21, the petition must be a form approved by the Administrative Office of the Courts, and is usually supplied by the clerk of court. Also, a fee of $125 will be charged to individuals seeking an expunction of a misdemeanor conviction that occurred before the age of 21. No fees are charged to the individual in any other expunction proceedings.

Section 7B-323 of the North Carolina Juvenile Code contains provisions for the expunction of reports alleging that an individual is guilty of child abuse and neglect. The statute is summarized below.

If an individual has been reported for child abuse or neglect, he or she may petition the court for an expunction of the abuse report within 30 days of the decision. A copy of the petition must be delivered to the Director of Social Services. The petition must contain the name, date of birth, and address of the individual. The petition also must name the juvenile who was the subject of the abuse determination and contain facts that give the court jurisdiction. If the individual fails to file a petition for expunction with in the 30-day time period, the individual waives the right to petition for expunction.

The court will set a date for a hearing on the petition and will notify the individual and the Director of Social Services. The Director has the burden of proving that the report of abuse is correct. Within 30 days after the hearing, the court will enter an order containing its findings. If the court determines that the Director failed to substantiate the report of abuse, the court will expunge the record.

Eligibility

In North Carolina, Article 5 of the Criminal Procedure Act provides a variety of circumstances in which an individual may be eligible for expunction. The procedure for obtaining an expunction varies, depending on the nature of the original disposition. Individuals who were charged with a crime but never convicted are eligible to petition the court for an order of expunction. In the case of an actual conviction, only individuals who received a pardon of innocence may petition for an expunction unless the conviction was a misdemeanor and the individual was under the age of 18 or the conviction was a misdemeanor possession of alcohol and the individual was under the age of 21.

Effect of Expunction

After receiving an order of expunction from the court, the individual is restored to the position he or she maintained before the arrest. The individual need not acknowledge a record that has been expunged in response to any inquiry made for any purpose. The Administrative Office of the Courts maintains a confidential file containing the names of individuals granted expungement for the purpose of determining whether an individual has previously been granted an expungement.

Expunction for Juveniles

Section 7B-3200 of the North Carolina Juvenile Code outlines the circumstances in which an individual may be eligible to petition the court for an order expunging his or her juvenile records. The statute is summarized below.

> If an individual was adjudicated undisciplined, he or she may petition the court for expunction of the records after reaching the age of 18.

> If an individual was adjudicated delinquent, he or she may petition the court for expunction of the records after reaching the age of 18, if the offense would not have been a Class A, B1, B2, C, D, or E felony if committed by an adult, at least 18 months have passed since the individual was released from custody or supervision, and he or she has not been convicted of any criminal offense in that time.

> The petition for expunction must contain the following:

> 1. An affidavit by the individual that he or she has been of good behavior and has not been convicted subsequently of any criminal offenses;

> 2. Verified affidavits of two people not related to the individual that the

individual is of good character; and

3. A statement that the petition is a motion in the case for which the individual was convicted.

The petition must be served upon the district attorney who will have an opportunity to object to the petition.

The court will conduct a hearing on the petition and if the court determines that the individual has been on good behavior, is free of any other convictions, and meets all of the eligibility requirements, the court will order the record expunged.

Other Remedies

Article III, Section V of the North Carolina Constitution gives the Governor the power to grant pardons for criminal convictions. Individuals must submit their applications for pardon to the Governor in writing and the application must be accompanied by a statement of reasons and a copy of the indictment. Typically, an individual must wait at least five years after completing his or her sentence before becoming eligible to apply for a pardon. Only an unconditional pardon will enable an individual to petition for expunction. The Governor's Executive Clemency Office accepts and investigates all pardon applications.

Governor's Executive Clemency Office contact information:

(919) 715-1695
Governor's Clemency Office
4294 Mail Service Center
Raleigh, NC 27699

Conclusion

In North Carolina, the statutes provide only limited relief from an actual criminal conviction. Regardless of the offense an individual is seeking to expunge, however, the process is complicated and should not be attempted without the help of an experienced attorney.

As we have said multiple times throughout this book "DO NOT TRY THIS AT HOME." There are tons of pitfalls and perils for those trying to obtain an expunction on their own without the help of an attorney. We've said it before and we'll say it now, ***do not try a do it yourself expunction.***

The primary problem is "do it yourselfers" can stir up a long dormant and as of yet un-pursued case. In other words, if you go making haphazard inquiries in the wrong case you can arouse prosecutorial interest and fire up an investigation of you and your case/arrest. Thus, use the resource section of our website at www.ultimatesecondchance.com/resources to help find an attorney in your area.

NORTH DAKOTA

Introduction

In North Dakota, little statutory authority authorizing the expunction of criminal records exists. The Uniform Controlled Substances Act is the only legislation that provides for the expunction of an actual criminal conviction. Other statutory authority for expunction is non-existent but the court has the inherent authority to expunge the record of an individual who was wrongfully arrested.

The Law in North Dakota

In North Dakota, there is very little statutory authority concerning the expunction of arrest records. One court case illustrates the inherent authority of courts to expunge arrest records when individuals are wrongfully arrested. That case, State v. Howe, stands for the principle that the court has an obligation to expunge arrest records of individuals who were not convicted and those who were wrongfully arrested. No constitutional right of privacy entitles individuals to the expunction of valid arrest records.

Section 19-03.1-23 of the North Dakota Century Code is part of the Uniform Controlled Substances Act. This is the only statute in the State which provides for the expungement of a criminal conviction. The pertinent part of the statute is summarized below.

> If an individual is convicted for the possession of one ounce or less of marijuana, and it is the individual's first offense, the court may expunge the record of the offense if a period of two years have passed since the conviction and the individual has not been convicted of any other criminal offense.

Eligibility

The ability to obtain the expunction of a criminal conviction is virtually non-existent in North Dakota. Other than a first-time offender convicted for possession of marijuana in an amount of one ounce or less, only individuals who were never convicted and wrongfully arrested are eligible for expunction.

Effect of Expungement

Both the statute and the case law are unclear as to the exact effect an expunction has on a criminal record. Individuals who were wrongfully arrested are said to be exonerated.

Expungement for Juveniles

Chapter 27-20 of the North Dakota Century Code contains the Uniform Juvenile Court Act which contains provisions outlining the confidentiality of juvenile records. The Act also contains a provision for the destruction of records pursuant to an expunction order but does not provide a method for requesting expunction. The relevant parts of the Act are summarized below.

> All records of the juvenile court are closed to the public. Only limited governmental and law enforcement agencies may access juvenile records. Law enforcement records of a juvenile must be kept separate from the records of adults and the juvenile files may not be open to public inspection. The records may be inspected by limited governmental and law enforcement agencies.

> All juvenile records must be maintained according to rules and procedures established by the North Dakota supreme court.

> Upon the final destruction of the record, the proceedings are to be treated as if they never occurred. All references to the record must be deleted and the juvenile need not acknowledge the record upon any inquiry for any purpose.

Other Remedies

Section 12.1-32-07.1 of the North Dakota Century Code allows an individual to request the court to set aside a guilty verdict against him or her after successfully completing a term of probation. It is decision of the court whether or not to grant such a set-aside, and the set-aside, if granted, will not expunge or seal the record. The statute is summarized below.

> If an individual was placed on probation, and he or she successfully completes the terms and conditions of his or her probation, the court will issue the individual a final discharge from supervision. At that time, the court may allow the individual to withdraw his or her guilty plea and may set aside the verdict of guilty, dismissing the indictment. Before dismissing the indictment, the court may reduce a felony conviction to a misdemeanor.

Article V, Section 7 of the North Dakota Constitution gives the Governor the power to grant pardons for criminal convictions. A pardon will remove all disabilities resulting from a criminal conviction, but it will not expunge a conviction. Applications are reviewed by the Pardon Advisory Board, and the Board forwards its recommendations to the Governor.

Pardon Advisory Board contact information:

> (701) 328-6192
> Pardon Clerk
> Pardon Advisory Board
> P.O. Box 5521
> Bismarck, ND 58506

Conclusion

In North Dakota, the statutes provide very little relief from a criminal conviction in the form of expunction. Other avenues for relief, such as a set-aside may exist. Regardless of the type of relief sought, the process for obtaining it is complex and should not be attempted without the help of an experienced attorney.

As we have said multiple times throughout this book "DO NOT TRY THIS AT HOME." There are tons of pitfalls and perils for those trying to obtain an expunction on their own without the help of an attorney. We've said it before and we'll say it now, *do not try a do it yourself expunction.*

The primary problem is "do it yourselfers" can stir up a long dormant and as of yet un-pursued case. In other words, if you go making haphazard inquiries in the wrong case you can arouse prosecutorial interest and fire up an investigation of you and your case/arrest. Thus, use the resource section of our website at www.ultimatesecondchance.com/resources to help find an attorney in your area.

OHIO

Introduction

In Ohio, the statutes provide for relief from a criminal record in the form of an order sealing the record. The courts have the ability to grant a request to seal the record for arrests and even convictions, provided the individual requesting an order sealing his or her record meets certain statutory requirements.

The Law in Ohio

Section 2953.52 of the Ohio Code of Crimes and Procedure outlines the availability and method for obtaining an order to seal records for individuals who were found not guilty or had all charges against them dismissed. The statute is summarized below.

> If an individual is found not guilty of an offense or all the charges against him or her are dismissed, the individual may petition the court for an order to seal the records in the case. The individual may file the petition at any time after the court enters a verdict of not guilty or the prosecutor dismisses the charges. If the grand jury enters no bill against an individual, he or she may petition the court for an order to seal the records in the case any time

after two years have passed since the date the grand jury reported to the court that no bill would be entered.

After receiving the petition, the court will schedule a hearing and notify the prosecutor who may object to the petition before the date of the hearing.

At the hearing, the court will determine whether the individual's record meets the requirements to be sealed and whether any criminal proceedings are currently pending against the individual. If the prosecutor has filed an objection, the court will consider the reasons set forth by the prosecutor against granting the petition and weigh the interests of the individual in having his or her records sealed against the needs of the government to maintain the records. If the court determines, after reviewing all the information, that the individual deserves an order sealing his or her records, the court will issue such an order.

Section 2953.32 of the Ohio Code of Crimes and Procedure provides the opportunity for first-time offenders to obtain an order sealing the records of a conviction. The statute is summarized below.

If an individual who is a first-time offender was convicted of a felony offense, he or she may petition the court for the sealing of the conviction record after three years have passed since the individual's final discharge. A first-time offender was convicted of a misdemeanor offense, he or she may petition the court for the sealing of the conviction record after one year has passed since the individual's final discharge. An individual who was arrested for any misdemeanor offense and who effected a bail forfeiture, may apply to the court for the sealing of the record after one year has passed from the date of the bail forfeiture.

After receiving the petition, the court will schedule a hearing and notify the prosecutor who may object to the petition before the date of the hearing.

At the hearing, the court will determine whether the individual's record meets the requirements to be sealed and whether any criminal proceedings are currently pending against the individual. If the prosecutor has filed an objection, the court will consider the reasons set forth by the prosecutor against granting the petition and weigh the interests of the individual in having his or her records sealed against the needs of the government to maintain the records. If the court determines, after reviewing all the information, that the individual has been rehabilitated and deserves an order sealing his or her records, the court will issue such an order. The record may be considered, however, in the event the individual is prosecuted of a subsequent offense.

Eligibility

Ohio statutes limit the availability of an order sealing criminal records to individuals who were found not guilty, had all charges against them dismissed, or are first-time offenders. A petition requesting the sealing of records will not be considered until all proceedings, including appeals, have concluded and the individual has paid all outstanding court costs and has finally been discharged from probation.

Section 2953.36 of the Ohio Code of Crimes and Procedure lists specific convictions for which the sealing of records is not available. These convictions include the following:

1. Convictions subjecting the individual to a mandatory prison term;

2. Sexual offenses;

3. Violent offenses including a misdemeanor of the first degree or a felony;

4. Convictions in which the victim was under 18 years old and the offense is a misdemeanor of the first degree or a felony;

5. Convictions of a felony of the first or second

degree; and

6. Bail forfeitures in traffic cases.

Effect of Sealing of Records

In Ohio, if a court enters an order sealing a criminal record, the proceedings in the case are deemed never to have occurred. The individual is restored to all rights and privileges he or she enjoyed before the arrest, and he or she is not required to acknowledge the existence of the sealed record to any inquiry for any purpose. Records sealed according to the first-time offender statute, however, may be accessed by limited government and law enforcement agencies and used in subsequent criminal proceedings against the individual.

Sealing and Expungement for Juveniles

In Ohio, like most other states, the statutes provide greater relief for juvenile offenders. Section 2151.358 of the Ohio Code outlines the availability of the relief of sealing of records and expungement for juvenile offenders. The statute is summarized below.

> If a juvenile has been adjudicated a delinquent child, an unruly child, or a juvenile traffic offender and the Department of Youth Services unconditionally discharges the juvenile the Department must immediately notify the court of the discharge.

After two years have passed from the unconditional discharge of the juvenile, the court must do one of the following:

1. If the juvenile was adjudicated an unruly child, order the record sealed; or

2. If the juvenile was adjudicated a delinquent child for committing an offense other than murder or a sexual offense, or was adjudicated a juvenile traffic offender, order the record sealed or notify the juvenile of his or her right to have the record sealed.

Any time after two years have passed since his or her unconditional discharge from custody or supervision, a juvenile who was adjudicated a delinquent child for an offense other than murder or a sexual offense, or who has been adjudicated a juvenile traffic offender may petition the court for an order to seal the record.

After receiving the petition, the court will schedule a hearing and notify the prosecutor. At the hearing, if the court determines that the juvenile has been rehabilitated satisfactorily, the court may order the record sealed.

If a juvenile was charged with possession of alcohol and successfully completes a court ordered diversionary program, the court must order the juvenile's record sealed.

If a juvenile was arrested and charged with being a delinquent child or unruly child or a juvenile traffic offender but is adjudicated not guilty or has the charges dismissed he or she may petition the court for an expungement of the record. The juvenile may petition for expungement any time after adjudication of not guilty or the charges have been dismissed. The court can begin the expungement proceedings on its own without a petition. In the case of sealing records, the juvenile court will maintain a confidential copy of the records, but in the case of an expungement order, all records will be destroyed.

Other Remedies

Article III, Section 11 of the Ohio Constitution gives the Governor the power to grant pardons for criminal convictions. All applicants must submit their applications to the Adult Parole Authority which investigates all applications and forwards recommendation to the Governor. If an individual is successful in obtaining a pardon, he or she becomes eligible to have his or her records sealed.

Adult Parole Authority contact information:

(614) 728-1938
Ohio Adult Parole Authority
1050 Freeway Drive North
Columbus, OH 43229

Conclusion

In Ohio, the statutes provide limited opportunities for relief from a criminal record. Individuals with arrests and even criminal convictions may be eligible to obtain relief in the form of a court order sealing the record. The process for obtaining a court order is complex and should not be attempted without the help of an experienced attorney.

As we have said multiple times throughout this book "DO NOT TRY THIS AT HOME." There are tons of pitfalls and perils for those trying to obtain a sealing of records on their own without the help of an attorney. We've said it before and we'll say it now, *do not try a do it yourself petition for the sealing of records.*

The primary problem is "do it yourselfers" can stir up a long dormant and as of yet un-pursued case. In other words, if you go making haphazard inquiries in the wrong case you can arouse prosecutorial interest and fire up an investigation of you and your case/arrest. Thus, use the resource section of our website at www.ultimatesecondchance.com/resources to help find an attorney in your area.

OKLAHOMA

Introduction

In Oklahoma, the statutes provide relief from a criminal record in the form of a court order sealing the criminal record, also called expungement. Relief is available to individuals in a wide variety of circumstances.

The Law in Oklahoma

Section 19 of the Oklahoma Code of Criminal Procedure outlines the procedure for petitioning for the sealing of records, or expungement, in the district court. The statute is summarized below.

> If an individual meets the statutory eligibility requirements for expungement, he or she may petition the district court for the sealing of all or part of his criminal record.

> After receiving the petition, the court will schedule a hearing and notify the district attorney, the arresting agency, the Oklahoma State Bureau of Investigation, and any other person or agency that may have relevant information related to the individual's record.

> If the court finds that the harm to the

individual outweighs the public interest in maintaining the records, the court may order the records to be sealed. The court also may order relief short of sealing by limiting access to the records. The individual or any interested party may appeal the determination of the court.

Rules 14.1, 14.2, and 14.3 of Section XIV of the Appendix to the Oklahoma Rules of the Court of Criminal Appeals establish that after a district court has entered an order sealing records, the individual may petition for the expungement of the related criminal appellate records in the Criminal Court of Appeals. The rules are summarized below.

An individual who received an order sealing his or her criminal records may apply for the expungement of the related records of the Court of Criminal Appeals.

An individual seeking an expungement must file an Application for Expungement with the Clerk of the Court of Criminal Appeals. The application must state the category under which the individual was qualified to request expungement in the district court, the date the district court entered the order, and the scope of the order. The individual must also file a certified copy of the district court's expungement order with the Application.

Section 991c of the Oklahoma Code of Criminal Procedure, entitled "Deferred Sentence," establishes the availability of expungement for individuals granted a deferred judgment and placed on probation. The statute is summarized below.

> If an individual pleads guilty or *nolo contendere* to a criminal offense, the court may defer further proceedings without entering a judgment of guilt and place the individual in a probationary program subject to terms and conditions imposed by the court.

> After successfully completing the terms of the probationary program, the court will discharge the individual and expunge the plea of guilty or *nolo contendere* from the record.

Section 2-410 of the Oklahoma Statutes is part of the Uniform Controlled Dangerous Substances Act. The statute provides that an individual arrested for the possession of a controlled substance for the first may be eligible for expungement upon completing the terms of court-ordered probation. The statute is summarized below.

> If a court finds an individual guilty of the possession of a controlled substance, and the individual has not been previously convicted of such an offense, [the court may further defer proceeding without] entering a judgment of guilt and place the individual on probation subject to terms and conditions imposed by the

court.

After successfully completing the terms of the probationary program, the court will discharge the individual and expunge the plea of guilty or *nolo contendere* from the record.

Eligibility

In addition to the availability of expungement for deferred judgments and a first-time conviction for the possession of a controlled substance, Section 18 of the Oklahoma Code of Criminal Procedure outlines the circumstances in which an individual generally is eligible to petition the court for an order of expungement. The statute is summarized below.

1. An individual only may be eligible to file a motion for expungement if he or she falls into one of the following categories.

2. The individual was acquitted;

3. The appellate court reversed the individual's conviction and the charges against him or her were dismissed;

4. The court determined that the individual was factually innocent through the use of DNA evidence;

5. The individual was arrested and no

charges were filed within one year of his or her arrest, or all the charges were dismissed on the merits;

6. The statute of limitations expired and the prosecutor filed no new charges;

7. The individual was under 18 years old at the time of the offense and has received a full pardon;

8. The offense was a misdemeanor, and the individual has not been convicted of any other criminal offense at least ten years since the conviction;

9. The offense was a nonviolent felony, the individual received a full pardon for the offense, and the individual has not been convicted of any other criminal offense at least ten years since the conviction; or

10. The arrest or conviction was a result of identity fraud.

Effect of Expungement

In Oklahoma, after an individual receives an order from the court granting expungement, his or her criminal records are sealed, except for very basic identification information. The arrest or conviction that was expunged is deemed never to have existed, and the individual need never acknowledge the record upon any direct inquiry for any purpose. The records are not destroyed, however, and they may be inspected by certain law enforcement and government agencies or by order of the court.

Expungement for Juveniles

Section 7302-1.2 of the Oklahoma Juvenile Code, entitled "Confidential Juvenile Records," provides that many juvenile records are confidential and are not available for public inspection. Numerous exceptions to the confidentiality requirement exist. Section 7307-1.8 of the Oklahoma Juvenile Code, entitled "Expungement of Open Juvenile Court Records," provides that juveniles whose records are not confidential may petition the court for the expungement of that record. The statute is summarized below.

An individual whose juvenile record is not maintained confidentially may petition the court for an order to expunge the record if the individual has reached the age of 21 or older, has not been convicted of any adult criminal offense, no charges are currently pending against him or her, and he or she has paid all fines and completed all of the court-ordered requirements relating to the juvenile offense.

After receiving the petition, the court will schedule a hearing and notify the Department of Juvenile Justice, the Oklahoma State Bureau of Investigation, and any other person or agency that may have relevant information related to the individual's record.

If the court finds that the harm to the individual outweighs the public interest in maintaining the records, the court may order the records to be sealed. The court also may order relief short of sealing by limiting access to the records. The individual or any interested party may appeal the determination of the court.

Other Remedies

Article VI, Section 10 of the Oklahoma Constitution gives the Governor the power to grant pardons for criminal convictions. The Department of Corrections investigates all pardon applications and forwards the results of the investigation to the Pardon and Parole Board. The Board will review the investigation and send a recommendation to the Governor who may not grant a pardon without a favorable recommendation from the Board. A pardon does not result in expungement, but non-violent offenders may petition for expungement ten years after receiving a pardon.

Oklahoma Pardon and Parole Board contact information:
> (405) 427-8601
> Pardon and Parole Board
> 4040 N. Lincoln Boulevard, Suite 219
> Oklahoma City, OK 73105

Conclusion

In Oklahoma, the statutes provide for relief from a criminal background for individuals in a variety of situations. The statutes refer to the relief as both an order to seal the records as well as expungement. The process for obtaining relief is complicated and should not be attempted without the help of an experienced attorney.

As we have said multiple times throughout this book "DO NOT TRY THIS AT HOME." There are tons of pitfalls and perils for those trying to obtain an expungement on their own without the help of an attorney. We've said it before and we'll say it now, *do not try a do it yourself expungement.*

The primary problem is "do it yourselfers" can stir up a long dormant and as of yet un-pursued case. In other words, if you go making haphazard inquiries in the wrong case you can arouse prosecutorial interest and fire up an investigation of you and your case/arrest. Thus, use the resource section of our website at www.ultimatesecondchance.com/resources to help find an attorney in your area.

OREGON

Introduction

In Oregon, the statutes provide relief from a criminal record in the form of a court order setting aside the record. Such an order has the effect of sealing a criminal record. The statutes provide that several different types of criminal records may be sealed, including records of certain convictions.

The Law in Oregon

Section 137.225 of the Oregon Statutes, entitled "Order Setting Aside Conviction or Record of Arrest," outlines the eligibility requirements and procedure to follow when applying to the court for an order setting aside a criminal record. Most misdemeanor and minor felony convictions may be set aside after a certain waiting period. The statute is summarized below.

> If an individual was convicted of a criminal offense, he or she may move for a court order setting aside the conviction three years after the date of the conviction. If an individual was arrested, but no charges were filed against him or her, he or she may request a court order setting aside the record of the arrest one year after the date of the arrest, and an individual

who was acquitted or had all the charges against him or her dismissed may apply for an order setting aside the records immediately after the charges are dismissed or the acquittal is entered.

The individual must send a copy of the motion, a full set of fingerprints, and a check payable to the Department of State Police for $80 to the prosecuting attorney. The prosecuting attorney will notify the victim of the crime and also can challenge the motion. The information is forwarded also to the Department of State Police Bureau of Criminal Identification, which will conduct a fingerprint search and return the results to the prosecuting attorney.

After receiving the motion, the court will schedule a hearing, and if the court determines that the behavior of the individual from the date of his or her arrest or conviction warrants setting aside the conviction or the record, it will grant the motion.

Eligibility

In Oregon, the statutes limit the types of convictions that may be set aside. Most misdemeanor and minor felony offenses may be set aside. Criminal convictions that may be set aside include Class C felonies with the exception of child abuse. The criminal possession of narcotics or marijuana and crimes punishable as either a felony or a misdemeanor, with the exception of sex crimes also may be set aside. Misdemeanor offenses and violations of municipal ordinances also are eligible to be set aside. The statute also lists specific crimes that are not eligible to be set aside, including municipal traffic offenses and any offense committed within ten years of receiving a previous set aside.

Effect of Set-Aside

After the court has granted a motion to set aside a criminal record, the individual is deemed never to have been convicted or arrested, and the records relating to the offense are sealed. The individual does not have to acknowledge the record upon any direct inquiry for any purpose. The record, however, may be accessed with a court order when necessary and in the interests of justice.

Expunction for Juveniles

In Oregon, like many other states, the statutes provide greater relief for juvenile offenders. Section 419A.262 of the Oregon Juvenile Code provides for the expunction of juvenile records in certain circumstances. The statute is summarized below.

A juvenile may apply to the court for the expunction of his or her juvenile record. The application must include the names of the juvenile courts, juvenile departments, institutions and law enforcement agencies that the individual believes have possession of his or her records. Notice of the application must be sent to the district attorney who may object to the expunction. If the district attorney files an objection, the court must hold a hearing on the matter, but if the district attorney does not object, the court may grant the expunction without a hearing.

The court will expunge the record if the juvenile meets the following conditions.

1. Five years have passed since the juvenile was terminated from supervision;

2. The juvenile has not been convicted of a felony or a Class A misdemeanor in that time;

3. There are no current juvenile court proceedings pending against the juvenile;

4. The juvenile is not before the juvenile court because he or she cannot be controlled by his or her parents or guardian, his or her behavior endangers others, or he or she has run away; and

5. The Juvenile Department does not know of any pending investigation into the conduct of the juvenile by a law enforcement agency.

If the individual has not met the requirements, the court still may order the expunction of an individual's juvenile record if it finds expunction would be in the best interests of the individual and the public. If an expunction is granted, the records are to be sealed and may eventually be destroyed after three years from the date the expunction was granted.

Other Remedies

Article V, Section 14 of the Oregon Constitution gives the Governor the power to grant pardons for criminal convictions. An individual must file an application for a pardon with the Governor's office and send copies of the application to the District Attorney, State Board of Parole and Post-Prison Supervision, and the Department of Corrections. The Governor interviews all pardon applicants personally before making his or her decision.

Oregon Office of the Governor contact information:

(503) 378-6246
Office of the Governor
160 State Capitol
900 Court St.
Salem, OR 97301

Conclusion

In Oregon, the statutes provide relief from a criminal record in the form of a court order granting the sealing of the record. Despite the fact that an order granting a sealing of the record may be obtained in various circumstances, including criminal convictions, the process is complex and should not be attempted without the help of an experienced attorney.

As we have said multiple times throughout this book "DO NOT TRY THIS AT HOME." There are tons of pitfalls and perils for those trying to obtain an expunction on their own without the help of an attorney. We've said it before and we'll say it now, *do not try a do it yourself expunction.*

The primary problem is "do it yourselfers" can stir up a long dormant and as of yet un-pursued case. In other words, if you go making haphazard inquiries in the wrong case you can arouse prosecutorial interest and fire up an investigation of you and your case/arrest. Thus, use the resource section of our website at www.ultimatesecondchance.com/resources to help find an attorney in your area.

PENNSYLVANIA

Introduction

In Pennsylvania, expungement of a criminal record occurs automatically upon the satisfaction of certain statutory requirements. For example, if an individual is acquitted, the arrest record automatically is expunged.

The Law in Pennsylvania

Under most circumstances, an individual need only be eligible for an order granting an expungement to receive one. Title 18, Section 9122 of the Pennsylvania Statutes outlines most of the eligibility requirements for automatic expungement. Other statutory provisions allow for expunction, both mandatory and discretionary.

Section 780-119 of the Health and Safety Chapter of the Pennsylvania Statutes, entitled "Expunging Criminal Records" is part of the Controlled Substance, Drug, Device, and Cosmetic Act. It provides that individuals arrested for violations of the Act but who are later acquitted, or have the charges against them dismissed or withdrawn, may have their criminal record expunged. This type of expungement is automatic, but is available only once for an individual.

Rule 320 of the Pennsylvania Rules of Criminal Procedure, entitled "Expungement Upon Successful

Completion of ARD Program," provides that an individual granted Accelerated Rehabilitative Disposition by the court may be eligible for mandatory expungement after satisfying the terms and conditions of the program. The rule is summarized below.

> If the judge orders the dismissal of the charges against an individual placed in an ADR program, the judge also must order the expungement of the individual's arrest record. The Attorney for the Commonwealth may object to the automatic expungement. In that event, the judge holds a hearing on the matter, allows all parties to be heard, and decides whether to grant the expungement.

Section 6341 of the Domestic Relations Chapter of the Pennsylvania Statutes, entitled "Amendment or Expunction of Information," outlines the procedures for obtaining the expungement of information contained in a report of child abuse filed with the Secretary of Public Welfare. This type of expungement is not mandatory. The statute is summarized below.

> At any time, the Secretary of Public Welfare may amend or expunge any record of suspected child abuse upon good cause shown after notifying the subjects of the report. An individual named in a report as a suspected perpetrator of child abuse can request the Secretary amend or expunge a report on the ground that it is inaccurate within 45 days of

being notified of the report.

If the Secretary grants the request, the Secretary must notify county agencies and law enforcement officials. County officials may file an administrative appeal with the Secretary, in which case a hearing will be conducted on the matter. All parties are allowed to be heard, and the Secretary will make a final decision whether to expunge the record.

If the Secretary refuses to grant the request, the individual may request a hearing on the matter within 45 days from the date of the refusal.

Eligibility

Section 9122 of the Crimes and Offenses Chapter of the Pennsylvania Statutes, entitled "Expungement," outlines the circumstances under which an individual may be eligible for expungement. The statute is summarized below. Expungement under this statute occurs automatically.

An individual is eligible for an automatic expungement of his or her criminal history information in the following circumstances:

1. No disposition was received within 18 months after the individual was arrested, and the court certifies that no disposition is available and no action is pending;

2. A court order requires the nonconviction data to be expunged;

3. The individual was convicted of a minor in possession offense, has since reached the age of 21, and has satisfied all the terms and conditions imposed by the court for the conviction;

4. The individual has reached the age of 70 and has not been arrested or prosecuted for ten years since his or her release from custody or supervision;

5. The individual has been dead for three years.

Expungement is not available for any crimes involving a sexual offense where the victim was under the age of 18.

Effect of Expungement

After the court has expunged an individual's criminal record, it is as if the arrest or proceedings never happened. The individual need not acknowledge the arrest or conviction in response to any inquiry for any purpose.

Expungement for Juveniles

Section 9123 of the Crimes and Offenses Chapter of

the Pennsylvania Statutes, entitled "Juveniles Records" outlines the circumstances in which the court may allow the expungement of a juvenile's criminal record. The statute is summarized below.

If a juvenile was adjudicated delinquent, the court may, on its own or on a motion of the juvenile expunge the record of delinquency if it finds one of the following:

1. The complaint was not substantiated or was dismissed by the court;

2. Six months have passed since the juvenile was finally discharged from supervision under a consent decree and no charges are pending against him or her;

3. Five years have passed since the juvenile was finally discharged from commitment, placement, or probation and he or she has not been convicted of a felony, misdemeanor, or adjudicated delinquent in that time, and no proceedings are pending against him or her; or

4. The juvenile has since turned 18 and the court orders the expungement after considering the nature of the offense, the juvenile's age and

character, adverse consequences he or she may suffer if the record is not expunged, and whether the record should be kept for the protection of the public safety.

Rule 170 of the Pennsylvania Rules of Juvenile Court Procedure, entitled "Expunging or Destroying Juvenile Court Records," outlines the procedure to follow if a juvenile decides to request expungement in his or her own behalf. The rule is summarized below.

Juvenile records can be expunged upon motion to the court. The motion must be in the form of a proposed court order and must contain the following information:

1. The juvenile's name;

2. The juvenile's date of birth;

3. The docket number of the juvenile's case;

4. The charges the juvenile seeks to expunge;

5. The law enforcement agency that initiated the charges;

6. The reference number of the police report the juvenile seeks to expunge;

7. The date of the arrest;

8. The disposition in the case;

9. The reasons for expunging the document; and

10. The agencies where the order to expunge should be sent.

The motion also must be sent to the chief juvenile probation officer, and the Attorney for the Commonwealth. If the Attorney for the Commonwealth does not consent to the expungement, the court will conduct a hearing on the matter and decide whether to grant the motion for expungement.

Other Remedies

Article IV, Section 9 of the Pennsylvania Constitution gives the Governor the power to grant pardons for criminal offenses, but the Governor may not act without a favorable recommendation from the Board of Pardons. The Board of Probation and Parole investigates all applications and the Board of Parole determines whether to grant a hearing based on the results of the investigation. Once an individual has received a pardon from the Governor, he or she becomes eligible for expungement.

Pennsylvania Board of Pardons contact information:

(717) 787-8125
Executive Secretary Board of Pardons
333 Market St., 15th Fl.
Harrisburg, PA 17126

Conclusion

In Pennsylvania, expungement occurs automatically in most circumstances. In some instances, government agencies may object to an order of expungement. In that situation, the court will conduct a hearing. The process of defending yourself in a hearing before the court can be daunting and should not be attempted without the help of an experienced attorney.

As we have said multiple times throughout this book "DO NOT TRY THIS AT HOME." There are tons of pitfalls and perils for those trying to obtain an expungement on their own without the help of an attorney. We've said it before and we'll say it now, *do not try a do it yourself expungement.*

The primary problem is "do it yourselfers" can stir up a long dormant and as of yet un-pursued case. In other words, if you go making haphazard inquiries in the wrong case you can arouse prosecutorial interest and fire up an investigation of you and your case/arrest. Thus, use the resource section of our website at www.ultimatesecondchance.com/resources to help find an attorney in your area.

PUERTO RICO

Introduction

In Puerto Rico, the statutes provide for relief from a criminal record in the form of elimination. This relief is available for most types of convictions, provided that the individual remains free of subsequent convictions for a certain statutory time period. The waiting period varies depending on the type of conviction the individual is seeking to eliminate.

The Law in Puerto Rico

Section 1731 of the Puerto Rico Code of Criminal Procedure outlines the availability of elimination. Most types of criminal convictions may be eliminated from an individual's record, provided he or she meets all of the eligibility requirements set forth in the statute. The statute is summarized below.

> If an individual was convicted of a misdemeanor or a felony other than murder, voluntary manslaughter, robbery, incest, extortion, rape, sodomy, lewd and indecent acts, kidnapping, aggravated burglary, aggravated arson, sale or distribution of a controlled substance, sabotage to public

services, possession, use or sale of an automatic weapon, or any felony that arises due to the illegal possession or use of explosives, he or she can apply to the Court of First Instance of Puerto Rico for an order eliminating the conviction from his or her criminal record if all the following circumstances are met.

1. Six months have passed since the individual's last conviction, in the case of a misdemeanor or non-violent felony offense, and he or she has not been convicted of any other offense in that time;

2. Five years have passed since the individual's last conviction, in the case of felony offense, and he or she has not been convicted of any other offense in that time; and

3. The individual has a good moral reputation in the community.

If the individual was convicted of one of the accepted felony offenses listed above, he or she may still be eligible to apply for elimination of that conviction from his or her record as long as 20 years have passed since the completion of his or her sentence, he or she has not been convicted of another offense in that time, and he or she has a good reputation in the community.

The court may, at its discretion, order the elimination of an offense from an individual's record after one year in the case of a misdemeanor and five years in the case of a felony, if the case is meritorious, the individual has served the sentence imposed, and the Secretary of the Department of Correction and Rehabilitation has granted a letter of reference to the individual. In these meritorious cases, if the District Attorney agrees to the elimination, no hearing will be held on the matter.

Section 2404 of the Laws of Puerto Rico provides that an individual with a conviction for the simple possession of narcotics or marijuana who had been placed on probation by the court and who has successfully completed his or her probation may be eligible for acquittal and the elimination of the offense from his or her public record. The statute is summarized below.

If an individual is convicted for the simple possession of narcotic drugs, marijuana, or stimulant or depressant substances for the first time, the court may accept a plea of guilty without entering a verdict of guilty and defer further proceedings and place the individual on probation. When the individual successfully completes all the terms and conditions of the probation imposed by the court, the court may, after a hearing, acquit the individual and dismiss the proceedings against him or her. This type of relief is available only one time for any individual.

Eligibility

In Puerto Rico, most types of criminal convictions may be eliminated once the statutory waiting period has run. Even an individual with a murder conviction may eventually have that conviction eliminated from his or her record after a period of 20 years have passed since the completion of his or her sentence. Only certain violations of the Puerto Rico Vehicle and Traffic Act may be eligible for elimination, however. Those violations include convictions for leaving the scene of an accident, reckless misconduct or wanton negligence in the operation of a motor vehicle, and driving under the influence.

Effect of Expungement

The statute does not discuss the effect of an order granting elimination for a general misdemeanor or felony conviction. Once charges against an individual are dismissed upon the successful completion of probation for a first-time drug possession offense, the record becomes confidential and only may be used by the court in subsequent criminal proceedings. Acquittal and dismissal are not considered a conviction.

Expungement for Juveniles

In Puerto Rico, no separate statutes exist regarding the elimination of juvenile criminal records. A juvenile may be eligible for elimination under the general elimination statutes.

Other Remedies

Article IV, Section 4 of the Puerto Rico Constitution gives the Governor the sole power to grant pardons for criminal convictions. The Puerto Rico Corrections Department investigates all applications. That Department passes the results of the investigation on to the Puerto Rico Board of Parole which makes a recommendation concerning the application to the Governor.

Puerto Rico Board of Parole contact information

(787) 754-8115 ext. 227
Chair, Puerto Rico Board of Parole
P.O. Box 40945, Minillas Station
San Juan, PR 00940

Conclusion

In Puerto Rico, the statutes provide relief from a criminal conviction in the form of elimination. Although elimination is available for most types of criminal convictions, the process of obtaining an order granting elimination is complex and should not be attempted without the help of an experienced attorney.

As we have said multiple times throughout this book "DO NOT TRY THIS AT HOME." There are tons of pitfalls and perils for those trying to obtain an expungement on their own without the help of an attorney. We've said it before and we'll say it now, *do not try a do it yourself elimination.*

The primary problem is "do it yourselfers" can stir up a long dormant and as of yet un-pursued case. In other words, if you go making haphazard inquiries in the wrong case you can arouse prosecutorial interest and fire up an investigation of you and your case/arrest. Thus, use the resource section of our website at www.ultimatesecondchance.com/resources to help find an attorney in your area.

RHODE ISLAND

Introduction

In Rhode Island, the statutes provide relief from a criminal record in the form of both expungement and the sealing of the record. An order sealing a record is available only to individuals who do not receive a criminal conviction for their charges. Expungement, however, may be available in the event of an actual conviction.

The Law in Rhode Island

Section 12-1-12 of the Rhode Island Code of Criminal Procedure provides that individuals who were arrested but never charged with a criminal offense and individuals who were charged with a criminal offense but later acquitted or had all charges against them dismissed, may petition the court for an order sealing all the records related to the offense. The statute is summarized below.

> If an individual was acquitted, all charges were dismissed against him or her, he or she otherwise was exonerated of all charges, or he or she was never charged in the first place, all identifying information must be destroyed within 60 days of the acquittal, dismissal or exoneration, and the criminal record must be sealed if the individual has no previous felony convictions.

Section 12-1-12.1 of the Rhode Island Code of Criminal Procedure provides the method for requesting an order sealing criminal records in the above situation. The statute is summarized below.

> If an individual was acquitted, all charges were dismissed, or he or she was exonerated of all charges in a criminal case, he or she can file a motion for the sealing of his or her record. An individual with a previous felony conviction is not eligible to file a motion for the sealing of his or her record.

> After receiving the motion, the court schedule a hearing, and the individual must send notice of the hearing to the Department of the Attorney General and the Police Department at least ten days before the hearing.

> If the court determines that the individual is entitled to the sealing of his or her criminal records, it will grant the motion and order the records sealed.

Section 12-1.3-2 of the Rhode Island Code of Criminal Procedure, entitled "Motion for Expungement," provides that first-time offenders may apply to the court for an order to expunge a criminal conviction after a specified waiting period. The statute is summarized below.

If an individual is convicted of a misdemeanor or a non-violent felony offense for the first time, he or she can file a motion for the expungement of his or her conviction in the court in which he or she was convicted.

An individual with a misdemeanor conviction must wait a period of five years from the completion of his or her sentence before filing a motion for expungement, and an individual with a non-violent felony conviction must wait a period of ten years from the completion of his or her sentence before filing a motion for expungement with the court.

Section 12-1.3-3 of the Rhode Island Code of Criminal Procedure outlines the procedure a first-time offender must follow when requesting an order granting expungement from the court. The statute is summarized below.

After receiving the motion, the court schedule a hearing, and the individual must send notice of the hearing to the Department of the Attorney General and the Police Department at least ten days before the hearing.

The court may grant the motion for expungement if it finds the individual meets the following requirements:

1. The individual has not been convicted of another offense in the five-year

waiting period for misdemeanor convictions or the ten-year waiting period for felony convictions;

2. No charges are currently pending against the individual;

3. The individual has exhibited good moral character during the required waiting period;

4. The individual has been rehabilitated; and,

5. The expungement of the individual's criminal record is consistent with the public interest.

If the court decides to grant the motion for expungement, it will order all records relating to the conviction expunged.

There are other statutes in the Rhode Island General Laws that permit expungement for specific types of criminal violations. For example, Section 3-8-12 of the Rhode Island General Laws relate to the regulation of alcohol sales. It provides that individuals between the ages of 18 and 21 who were convicted of the illegal possession of alcohol may have that conviction expunged. The statute is summarized below.

If an individual is convicted of a violation for unlawful drinking, misrepresentation of age with false identification for the purpose of unlawful drinking, transportation of alcoholic beverages by an underage person, or possession of alcohol by an underage person, the court records of that conviction must be expunged if the individual was between the ages of 18 and 21 at the time of the conviction.

Section 31-41.1-10 of the Rhode Island Motor and Other Vehicles Code, entitled "Expungement," provides that any violation of the Motor and Other Vehicles Code must be expunged after three years have passed since the violation.

Eligibility

In Rhode Island, an individual is eligible to receive an order sealing his or her criminal record only if he or she was never charged for his or her arrest, all the charges against him or her were dismissed, or he or she eventually was acquitted or exonerated of all charges. An individual with a criminal conviction may still, however, receive an order granting expungement of the conviction, provided he or she satisfies certain statutory requirements during a designated waiting period. Alcohol related offenses may be expunged for individuals between the ages of 18 to 21, and all motor vehicle violations are automatically expunged after the passage of three years. Any charges of domestic violence, regardless of the outcome of the case, are subject to a three-year waiting period before they are eligible for sealing or expungement.

Effect of Expungement

If a court enters an order sealing a criminal record, the record eventually may be physically destroyed. An expunged record, however, may not be destroyed and may be accessed in the event the individual is charged with a subsequent criminal offense. Also, in the case of an expungement, the individual must disclose the fact of the conviction if he or she is applying for employment with certain government agencies.

Expungement for Juveniles

In Rhode Island, no statutes permit expungement for juvenile offenders. Instead, juvenile records are given special status. Section 14-1-40 of the Rhode Island General Laws pertains to delinquent and dependent children and it provides that juvenile adjudications do not have the effect of a conviction, and they cannot be used to impose any disabilities upon the juvenile. The statute is summarized below.

A juvenile adjudication may not impose any disabilities that ordinarily result from a conviction upon a child. A child is not considered a criminal due to a juvenile adjudication. Prosecutors may not use juvenile adjudications as evidence against a child in any proceeding in any court, and juvenile adjudications may not disqualify a child for any future civil service application, examination, or appointment.

If a juvenile was found delinquent for an act that would constitute a felony if committed by an adult, the record is available to the Attorney General for future sentencing considerations.

Other Remedies

Article IX, Section 13 of the Rhode Island Constitutions gives the Governor the power to grant pardons for criminal convictions. No eligibility requirements exist for requesting a pardon, and no formal process to follow exists when making a request. The Governor's pardon power is subject to the Rhode Island Senate's review and consent. For more information contact the Special Counsel to the Governor.

Special Counsel to the Governor contact information:

(401) 222-8114
Office of the Governor
222 State House
Providence, RI 02903

Conclusion

In Rhode Island, the statutes provide for relief from a criminal conviction in the form of a court order granting expungement. The decision to grant such an order is completely within the court's discretion. The process is complex and should not be attempted without the help of an experienced attorney.

As we have said multiple times throughout this book "DO NOT TRY THIS AT HOME." There are tons of pitfalls and perils for those trying to obtain an expungement on their own without the help of an attorney. We've said it before and we'll say it now, *do not try a "do it yourself expungement."*

The primary problem is "do it yourselfers" can stir up a long dormant and as of yet un-pursued case. In other words, if you go making haphazard inquiries in the wrong case you can arouse prosecutorial interest and fire up an investigation of you and your case/arrest. Thus, use the resource section of our website at www.ultimatesecondchance.com/resources to help find an attorney in your area.

SOUTH CAROLINA

Introduction

In South Carolina, the statutes provide for relief from a criminal record in the form of a court order granting expungement. An expungement is available only to a limited class of individuals, and does not destroy a criminal record. An individual who is found innocent of a charge against him or her, however, may be entitled to the destruction of the record relating to that charge.

The Law in South Carolina

Section 22-5-910 of the Code of Laws of South Carolina, entitled "Expungement of Criminal Records," provides that first-time offenders convicted in the magistrate or municipal court may apply to those courts for an order expunging the record of the offense after a certain period of time. The statute is summarized below.

> If an individual was convicted as a first-time offender in a magistrate or municipal court, he or she may apply to the court for an order expunging the record of the conviction after three years have passed from the date of the conviction.

> Expungement under this statute is not available for offenses involving the operation of a motor

vehicle; offenses involving fish, game, and watercraft; or offenses involving criminal domestic violence. A first offense for criminal domestic violence conviction may be expunged five years after the date of conviction.

If the individual has not been convicted of another offense during the applicable waiting period, the court may order expungement of the conviction. This type of expungement is available to an individual only once.

Section 17-1-40 of the South Carolina Code of Criminal Procedure provides for the automatic destruction of all records relating to a charge which was eventually dismissed or a charge for which the individual was found not guilty. The statute is summarized below.

If an individual was charged with a criminal offense but the charge later has been dismissed or the individual was found not guilty, the records of the arrest must be destroyed.

Section 44-53-450 of the Code of Laws for South Carolina provides that a first-time offender charged with the possession of marijuana or a controlled substance may have all the charges against him or her dismissed if he or she successfully completes a probationary program. Individuals under the age of 25 at the time of the offense may have their record expunged. The statute is summarized below.

If an individual is convicted as a first-time offender for the possession of marijuana, or a controlled substance, the court may defer the proceedings against the individual without entering a guilty judgment and place the individual on probation.

If an individual successfully completes all the terms and conditions of probation, the court will discharge the individual from probation and dismiss the proceedings against him or her. An individual is eligible for discharge and dismissal only once.

If the individual was under the age of 25 at the time of the offense, he or she may apply to the court for an order expunging the record of the offense. The court will conduct a hearing and if the court determines the individual was discharged from probation, the charges were dismissed, and the individual was under the age of 25 at the time of the offense, will enter an order for expungement.

Section 22-5-920 of the Code of Laws of South Carolina, entitled "Conviction as a Youthful Offender," provides that a one-time youthful offender may apply to the court for an expungement of the record of the conviction. A "youthful offender" is an individual under the age of 21. The statute is summarized below.

After an individual's first offense as a youthful offender, he or she may apply to the circuit court for an order expunging the record of the conviction after 15 years have passed since the date of the conviction. If the individual has no other convictions during that 15-year period, the court may grant the request for expungement. An individual is eligible for this type of expungement only once.

Eligibility

In South Carolina, a first-time offender may apply with the court for the expungement of a magistrate or municipal court conviction after a certain time period. First-time offenders charged with the possession of marijuana or a controlled substance also may be eligible for expungement if they were under 25 at the time of the offense and they successfully complete a probationary program. Individuals under the age of 21 may have a first-time conviction expunged after a period of 15 years. Also, as with most states, South Carolina provides that individuals against whom all charges are dismissed or who are found not guilty of such charges are entitled to expungement.

Effect of Expungement

After the court grants an order for expungement, the record of the offense is no longer available to the public, but may be used in subsequent criminal proceedings. The individual need not acknowledge the record in response to any question for any purpose. If an individual received an expungement because the charges against him or her were dismissed or he or she was found not guilty of the offense, the record may be destroyed.

Expungement for Juveniles

Section 63-19-2050 of the South Carolina Children's Code, entitled "Petition for Record Destruction" provides that a non-violent juvenile offender may petition for the destruction of his or her juvenile record if he or she has since reached the age of 18 without any subsequent adjudications. The statute is summarized below.

> A juvenile who was taken into custody, charged with delinquency, or adjudicated delinquent for a non-violent offense, may petition the court for an order destroying the records of the offense. The decision to grant the order for destruction is entirely within the discretion of the court. The juvenile must have reached the age of 18; successfully completed the sentences imposed by the court, and not have been charged with a subsequent criminal offense to be eligible to petition the court for such an order. A juvenile with a previous adjudication for an offense that would impose a maximum jail term of five or more years if committed as an adult, is not eligible to petition the court for the destruction of the record. Also, any adjudication for a violent crime may not be expunged.

If the court grants the motion for expungement, the record must be destroyed.

Other Remedies

Article IV, Section 14 of the South Carolina Constitution gives the Governor the power to grant reprieves and commute death sentences. The power to pardon is granted statutorily to the Probation, Parole, and Pardon Board. The Board conducts a hearing on all pardon applications it receives before determining whether to grant the relief of a pardon.

South Carolina Probation, Parole, and Pardon Board contact information:

(803) 734-9267
Department of Probation, Parole and Pardon Services
2221 Devine Street, Suite 600
P.O. Box 50666
Columbia, SC 29250

Conclusion

South Carolina provides for relief from a criminal record in the form of a court order granting expungement. Not all individuals are eligible to apply to the court for such an order. The process of applying to the court for an order granting expungement is complex and should not be attempted without the help of an experienced attorney.

As we have said multiple times throughout this book "DO NOT TRY THIS AT HOME." There are tons of pitfalls and perils for those trying to obtain an expungement on their own without the help of an attorney. We've said it before and we'll say it now, *do not try a do it yourself expungement.*

The primary problem is "do it yourselfers" can stir up a long dormant and as of yet un-pursued case. In other words, if you go making haphazard inquiries in the wrong case you can arouse prosecutorial interest and fire up an investigation of you and your case/arrest. Thus, use the resource section of our website at www.ultimatesecondchance.com/resources to help find an attorney in your area.

SOUTH DAKOTA

Introduction

In South Dakota, the statutes provide for relief from a criminal record in the form of an expungement. Expungement in South Dakota amounts to the judicial sealing of a criminal record, meaning the record is not available for public inspection.

The Law in South Dakota

Sections 23A-27-13 and 23A-27-14 of the South Dakota Code of Criminal Procedure provide that the record of a first-time offender is expunged automatically after the successful completion of probation. The statutes are summarized below.

> If an individual is found guilty of a misdemeanor or a felony offense, which is not punishable by death or life in prison, for the first time, the court may suspend the imposition of the sentence and place the individual on probation.
>
> If the individual successfully completes all the terms and conditions of the probation set by the court, the court will discharge the individual and dismiss all charges against him

or her. Discharge and dismissal under these statutes may be granted only once to an individual.

Eligibility

In South Dakota, only first-time offenders guilty of a crime that is not punishable by death or life in prison are eligible to have those records expunged. The individual first must have been granted a suspended sentence by the court and must have successfully completed that sentence before the sealing will take effect.

Effect of Expungement

After the court has granted an order expunging a criminal record, it is as if the offense never occurred. The record is sealed and may not be accessed by the public. The record may, however, be used by the court in any subsequent criminal proceedings.

Sealing of Records for Juveniles

Section 26-7A-115 of the South Dakota Laws pertaining to juvenile records provides the judicial sealing of records for individuals who were declared juvenile delinquents. The statute is summarized below.

If a juvenile has been the subject of a juvenile delinquency proceeding, he or she may petition the court for an order sealing the record. The petition will not be considered by the court until at least one year has passed since the juvenile was released from supervision.

After receiving a petition, the court will schedule a hearing and send notice to the state's attorney and any other person with relevant information concerning the juvenile.

The court may order sealed all of the court's records and files in the custody or under the control of any other agency or official if the court finds that the juvenile has not been adjudicated delinquent since the original proceeding, no proceedings are pending against the juvenile, and the juvenile has been rehabilitated.

Other Remedies

There are two distinct types of pardons in South Dakota. Article IV, Section 3 of the South Dakota Constitution gives the Governor the power to independently grant pardons for criminal convictions. Sections 24-14-1 and 24-14-8 of the South Dakota laws provide that the Governor may seek the advice of the Board of Pardons Paroles or the Board of Pardons and Paroles may make recommendations to the Governor involving first-time offender, exceptional pardons. First-time offenders must wait five years from the completion of their sentence before applying for an exceptional pardon. If an individual receives either type of pardon, he or she becomes eligible for the judicial sealing of the record.

South Dakota Board of Pardons and Paroles contact information:

(605) 367-5040
South Dakota Board of Pardons and Paroles
South Dakota State Penitentiary
1600 North Drive
P.O. Box 5911
Sioux Falls, SD 57117

Conclusion

In South Dakota, the statutes provide for relief from a criminal record in the form of a judicial sealing of the record. Adult judicial sealing are automatic, but juvenile judicial sealing may require a court order. The process of obtaining a judicial sealing is complex and should not be attempted without the help of an experienced attorney.

As we have said multiple times throughout this book "DO NOT TRY THIS AT HOME." There are tons of pitfalls and perils for those trying to obtain an expungement on their own without the help of an attorney. We've said it before and we'll say it now, *do not try a do it yourself expungement*.

The primary problem is "do it yourselfers" can stir up a long dormant and as of yet un-pursued case. In other words, if you go making haphazard inquiries in the wrong case you can arouse prosecutorial interest and fire up an investigation of you and your case/arrest.

Thus, use the resource section of our website at www.ultimatesecondchance.com/resources to help find an attorney in your area.

TENNESSEE

Introduction

In Tennessee, the statutes provide relief from a criminal record in the form of a court order granting expungement of the record. When a criminal record is expunged, the contents of the record become confidential and may not be accessed by the public. If an individual is found not guilty of a criminal offense, the record may be physically destroyed.

The Law in Tennessee

Section 40-32-101 of the Tennessee Code of Criminal Procedure provides that an individual who does not receive a criminal conviction is entitled to the destruction of the records relating to the offense. The statute is summarized below.

> If an individual was arrested for a felony or misdemeanor offense, but never was charged for the offense, any charges were later dismissed, the individual was found not guilty, or the court entered a judgment of *nolle prosequi*, he or she may petition the court to destroy the records of the arrest without cost. If the charges against the individual were dismissed due the successful completion of a diversion program, the individual will be

assessed a fee for the destruction of the record. A record may not be destroyed if the charges stemmed from a sexual offense. Likewise, the record of an individual with a previous conviction may not be destroyed.

Section 40-35-313 of the Tennessee Code of Criminal Procedure provides that an individual granted probation for a criminal offense may petition for the expungement of his criminal record after the successful completion of all the terms and conditions of his or her probation. The statute is summarized below.

If an individual is charged with a criminal offense, the court may defer further proceedings against the individual and place him or her on probation.

An individual is only eligible for probation if he or she was found not guilty or plead not guilty or *nolo contendere* to the charges, the charge was not a sexual offense or a Class A or B felony, and the individual has not been previously convicted of a Class A or B felony.

If an individual successfully completes all the terms and conditions of probation, the court will discharge the individual from probation and dismiss all the charges against him or her. A discharge due to the successful completion of probation is not considered as a conviction. The opportunity for probation is available only once for an individual.

After the individual is discharged from probation, he or she may petition the court for the expungement of his or her record, and the court will conduct a hearing on the matter. If the court determines that the individual was discharged from probation and all the charges against him or her were dismissed, the court will enter an order expunging the record.

Section 57-3-412 of the Tennessee Code provides that individuals under the age of 21 who are convicted of the illegal possession of alcohol may petition for the destruction of the record relating to the offense after the passage of a specified time period. The statute is summarized below.

If an individual under the age of 21 is convicted for the illegal possession or transportation of alcohol, he or she may request the record of the conviction be destroyed after six years have passed from the date of the offense.

Eligibility

In Tennessee, the statutes provide that an individual may receive the expungement of a felony record only if he or she never received a criminal conviction. To be free from conviction the individual must never have been charged with an offense, had all the charges against him or her dismissed, have been found not guilty of the offense, or successfully completed a court-ordered diversionary program. The illegal possession of alcohol by an individual under the age of 21 is classified as a misdemeanor offense, and the record of such a conviction may be destroyed after six years have passed from the date of the offense.

Effect of Expungement

After the court grants an order expunging the record of a criminal offense, it is as if the offense never took place. An individual need not acknowledge the records upon any direct inquiry for any purpose. The record of the offense becomes confidential, and is not available to the public. The record may be accessed, however, by courts and other law enforcement agencies in subsequent criminal or civil proceedings.

Expungement for Juveniles

Section 55-10-711 of the Tennessee Code is part of the Juvenile Offender Act, entitled "Expungement of Records". It provides that an individual under the age of 18 may petition for the destruction of any record pertaining to the suspension of his or her driver's license. The statute is summarized below.

> If a juvenile's driver's license was suspended, all records relating to that suspension must be expunged at the time the juvenile reaches the age of 18.

> The expungement of juvenile records for any other

type of offense is governed by the same statutes summarized above that govern the expungement of adult criminal records.

Other Remedies

Article III, Section 6 of the Tennessee Constitution gives the Governor the power to pardon criminal convictions. An individual is eligible to apply for a pardon if he or she has not received another conviction within five years from the completion of his or her sentence, has demonstrated good citizenship, and presents compelling need for a pardon. All applications are received by the Board of Probation and Parole. The Board conducts a hearing on the application and forwards its recommendation to the Governor. A pardon will not make an individual eligible for expungement.

Tennessee Board of Probation and Parole contact information:

> (615) 741-1673
> General Counsel
> State of Tennessee Board of
> Probation and Parole
> 404 James Robertson Parkway
> Nashville, TN 37243

Conclusion

In Tennessee, the statutes provide relief from a criminal record in the form of an order of expungement. An order of expungement is available only to a limited group of criminal offenders. The process of obtaining an order for expungement is complex and should not be attempted without the help of an experienced attorney.

As we have said multiple times throughout this book "DO NOT TRY THIS AT HOME." There are tons of pitfalls and perils for those trying to obtain an expungement on their own without the help of an attorney. We've said it before and we'll say it now, *do not try a do it yourself expungement*.

The primary problem is "do it yourselfers" can stir up a long dormant and as of yet un-pursued case. In other words, if you go making haphazard inquiries in the wrong case you can arouse prosecutorial interest and fire up an investigation of you and your case/arrest. Thus, use the resource section of our website at www.ultimatesecondchance.com/resources to help find an attorney in your area.

TEXAS

Introduction

In Texas, expunction allows for people wrongfully arrested and charged with a criminal offense due to false information, mistake, or other similar reasons to clear those records. Texas does not allow expunction for people who pled guilty or *nolo contendere* to a criminal offense and were placed on court ordered supervision or probation, including deferred adjudication. However, it is possible to seek an expunction of guilty and *nolo contendere* pleas to minor or petty crimes classified as Class "C" misdemeanors.

The Law in Texas

Texas allows for expunction only when all of the conditions set forth in the statute have been met. Article 55.01 of the Texas Code of Criminal Procedure, entitled "Right to Expunction" contains the conditions which must be satisfied in order to be eligible for the right of expunction. The statute is summarized below.

A person who has been placed under arrest for commission of a felony or misdemeanor is entitled to have all records and files relating to the arrest expunged if:

1. He or she has been tried and acquitted of the

offense. A person charged with several offenses arising out of the same episode must be acquitted of all of those offenses before that person becomes eligible for expunction.

2. He or she has been tried, convicted, and later pardoned for the offense.

A person also may seek expunction if all of the following conditions exist.

1. An indictment charging the person with a felony never was presented and the limitations period has expired; or the indictment was dismissed because the court found its presentment was due to mistake or other similar reasons;

2. The person was released, the charge is no longer pending, and it did not result in a conviction or court-ordered probation for any offense other than a Class C misdemeanor.; and

3. The person was not convicted of a felony in the five years before the arrest.

A person is entitled to have any information identifying him or her in the arrest records of another person expunged if:

The arrested person gave the information falsely, without consent, and that is the only reason the information became part of the record.

Expunction for Juveniles

Texas bestows the relief of expunction more readily upon juvenile offenders and the availability and eligibility requirements differ from the general conditions presented above. Article 45.0216 of the Texas Code of Criminal Procedure, entitled "Expunction of Certain Conviction Records of Children," contains the separate requirements for obtaining an expunction of criminal offenses committed under the age of 17. The statute is summarized below:

A person convicted of only one misdemeanor punishable by a fine (other than public intoxication) or the violation of a penal ordinance while he or she was a child, may request expunction from the court in which he or she was convicted after his or her 17th birthday. The request must meet certain requirements:

1. The request for expunction must be in writing and under oath;

2. The request must contain a statement by the person seeking expunction that he or she was not convicted of any offenses other than the one he or she seeks to expunge; and

3. The court requires the person requesting expunction to pay a $30 fee.

Eligibility

The Texas Code of Criminal Procedure makes the right to expunction somewhat of a catch all provision. Felony and misdemeanor charges, including DUIs and DWIs fall under the same statute requiring anyone seeking expunction to meet all of the conditions set forth above. The Code precludes the availability of expunction for a criminal conviction, no matter the type, unless the arrest or conviction resulted from mistake, misinformation, or other similar reasons.

Effect of the Expunction

After an order granting expunction becomes final, any release or use of the expunged records is strictly prohibited. The person granted expunction may deny the existence of the arrest as well as the expunction order itself.

Other Remedies

If an individual is not eligible for expunction in Texas, other remedies may be available that may eventually lead to the possibility of expunction. A full pardon restores certain rights forfeited as a result of a conviction, such as the right to serve on a jury and hold public office; and a full pardon will remove barriers to certain types of employment. A person who is convicted of a criminal offense and receives a full pardon is entitled to an expunction. The Executive Clemency Section of the Texas Board of Pardons and Paroles provides pardon application packets. Individuals may contact the

Executive Clemency Section to request a packet.

The Executive Clemency Section contact information:

(512) 406-5852
Texas Board of Pardons and Paroles
Executive Clemency Section
P.O. Box 13401, Capitol Station
Austin, TX 78711

Section 411.081(d) of the Texas Government Code contains another remedy: an order for non-disclosure. If the court places a person on deferred adjudication and later discharges and dismisses that person, he or she may petition the court for an order of non-disclosure by paying a fee after a certain conviction-free period determined by the statute and depending upon the nature of the crime. People convicted of felony offenses must go a period of five years without another criminal conviction before they can petition the court for an order of non-disclosure. An order of non-disclosure prevents a criminal justice agency from releasing the records to the public. The records may, however, still be released to other criminal justice agencies.

Texas Family Code Section 58.003 allows, for juveniles only, the court to order the sealing of the records if the court finds that two years have elapsed since the final discharge of the case and the juvenile has not been convicted of another crime. When the records have been sealed, for all purposes other than capital prosecution, the case is treated as if it never happened, and the person whose records have been sealed is never required to disclose it.

Conclusion

While the Texas Code of Criminal Procedure allows for an eligible person to file an ex parte expunction petition in the district court of the county where the arrest occurred, the courts require strict compliance with all of the conditions, and many people find the process extremely complex.

As we have said multiple times throughout this book "DO NOT TRY THIS AT HOME." There are tons of pitfalls and perils for those trying to obtain an expunction on their own without the help of an attorney. We've said it before and we'll say it now, *do not try a do it yourself expunction.*

The primary problem is "do it yourselfers" can stir up a long dormant and as of yet un-pursued case. In other words, if you go making haphazard inquiries in the wrong case you can arouse prosecutorial interest and fire up an investigation of you and your case/arrest. Thus, use the resource section of our website at www.ultimatesecondchance.com/resources to help find an attorney in your area.

UTAH

Introduction

In Utah, the statutes provide for the relief from a criminal record in the form of expungement. Expungement may be granted to individuals who were arrested for a criminal offense but never convicted. Expungement also may be available to seal certain types of criminal convictions.

The Law in Utah

Section 77-18-10 of the Utah Code of Criminal Procedure provides the eligibility requirements an individual must meet before petitioning the court for an order expunging the record of an arrest. The statute is summarized below.

> If an individual was arrested, he or she may petition the court for an order expunging the record of the arrest if 30 days have passed since the individual was arrested, the individual has not been arrested for another offense since the original arrest, and the arrest led to one of the following situations:

1. The individual was released without being charged;

2. The proceedings against the individual were dismissed;

3. The individual was discharged without conviction and no charges have been refiled within 30 days;

4. The individual was acquitted at trial; or

5. The record of any proceedings against the individual has been sealed.

If an individual seeks expungement because he or she was released without being charged, he or she may petition the court for an order of expungement before 30 days have passed since his or her arrest if extraordinary circumstances exist. The court will issue the expungement if, in the interests of justice, the order should be issued before the end of the 30-day waiting period.

In all other circumstances, if the individual meets all eligibility requirements, the Criminal Investigations and Technical Services Division of the Department of Public Safety will issue a certificate of eligibility. The individual must file the certificate with the prosecuting attorney and the court before the Division will enter an order of expungement. If the Division finds that the individual is eligible, it will issue an order granting expungement.

Section 77-18-11 of the Utah Code of Criminal Procedure provides for the expungement of certain criminal convictions. The statute is summarized below.

If an individual was convicted of a criminal offense, he or she may petition the court for an order expunging the record of the conviction. The individual must submit a certificate of eligibility issued by the Division along with the petition to the court. A copy of the certificate of eligibility also must be sent to the prosecuting attorney and the Department of Corrections. The Department will notify any victims of the crime about the expungement request.

If either the victim or the prosecuting attorney objects to the expungement, the court will conduct a hearing on the matter. Any individual with relevant information concerning the individual can speak at the hearing. If no objections are filed, the court may grant expungement order without a hearing.

Eligibility

In Utah, the statutes make expungement available for individuals who were arrested but never convicted, as well as individuals who received criminal convictions. The statute does, however, list certain types of criminal convictions that may not be expunged including capital felony, first degree felony, second degree forcible felony, any sexual act against a minor, and any registerable sexual offense.

Effect of Expungement

After the court has entered an order for expungement, the affected record is sealed and not available to the public for inspection. The records remain available, however, to limited governmental and law enforcement agencies. After receiving an order of expungement, it is as if the individual was never arrested. An individual need not acknowledge the existence of an expunged record in response to any direct inquiry.

Expungement for Juveniles

Section 78-3a-905 of the Utah Code is part of the Juvenile Court Act of 1996 and it outlines the procedure for requesting the expungement of a juvenile court record. The statute is summarized below.

An individual who was adjudicated as a juvenile may petition the juvenile court for expungement of that record once he or she has reached the age of 18, and one year has elapsed since the termination of the juvenile court's jurisdiction over the individual. The petition must include the original criminal history report from the Bureau of Criminal Identification. A copy of the petition also must be sent to the county attorney or district attorney.

After receiving the petition, the court will schedule a hearing and will notify the county or district attorney, any agencies with custody of the records, and any victims of the crime that is subject of the expungement request. Any of those individuals or agencies may testify at the hearing.

At the hearing, the court will consider the individual's conduct and the nature of the crime to determine whether the individual has been rehabilitated successfully. If the court finds that the individual has been rehabilitated successfully, it may issue the order of expungement if the individual has not been convicted of a felony or misdemeanor involving moral turpitude and no such actions are pending against the individual.

Juvenile court records involving crimes of aggravated murder or murder may not be expunged.

Rules 7-308 and 56 of the Utah Court Rules outline the process for obtaining an order of expungement from the juvenile court. The rules mirror statute 78-3a-905.

Other Remedies

Article VII, Section 12 of the Utah Constitution gives the Governor the power to grant pardons for criminal convictions. An individual is eligible to request a pardon once five years have passed since the termination of his or her sentence. The Board of Pardons and Paroles reviews all applications, but not all applicants will be granted a hearing before the Board. After voting on the application, the Board forwards its recommendation to the Governor.

The Utah Board of Pardons and Paroles contact information:

> (801) 261-6464
> Utah Board of Pardons and Paroles
> 448 East Winchester St., Suite 300
> Murray, UT 84107

Conclusion

In Utah, the statutes provide for the relief of expungement in a variety of circumstances. An order of expungement effectively may seal the records of a criminal conviction. The process of obtaining an order of expungement is complex and should not be attempted without the help of an experienced attorney.

As we have said multiple times throughout this book "DO NOT TRY THIS AT HOME." There are tons of pitfalls and perils for those trying to obtain an expungement on their own without the help of an attorney. We've said it before and we'll say it now, *do not try a "do it yourself expungement."*

The primary problem is "do it yourselfers" can stir up a long dormant and as of yet un-pursued case. In other words, if you go making haphazard inquiries in the wrong case you can arouse prosecutorial interest and fire up an investigation of you and your case/arrest. Thus, use the resource section of our website at www.ultimatesecondchance.com/resources to help find an attorney in your area.

VERMONT

Introduction

The law of Vermont allows for a judicial order granting expungement, or a judicial sealing. Individuals who successfully complete court-ordered probation or an adult court diversionary program may be granted such relief. In general, judges are allowed discretion over such orders.

The Law in Vermont

Title 13, Section 5413 of the Vermont Statutes, entitled "Expungement of Records," provides that individuals required to register as sex offenders are entitled to have their information removed from the registry if the conviction is reversed. The statute is summarized below.

> If an individual was convicted of a sex offense, but the conviction was reversed and dismissed, he or she is not required to register as a sex offender. Any information that was already placed in the sex offender registry must be removed and destroyed.

Title 13, Section 7041 of the Vermont Statutes, entitled "Deferred Sentence," provides that individuals who successfully complete court-ordered probation may have their criminal record expunged. The statute is summarized below.

An individual may be granted a deferred sentence and placed on probation by the court if the following conditions are met:

1. The individual is 28 years of age or younger;

2. The offense does not involve a type of offense known as a listed offense, generally a violent or sexual offense;

3. The court orders a pre-sentence investigation;

4. The court permits the victim to give a statement;

5. The court reviews the investigation and the victim's statement with the individual; and

6. Deferring sentence is in the interest of justice.

If the individual successfully completes the court-ordered probation, the court will strike the adjudication of guilt and discharge the individual.

Once the individual has been discharged, the record of the offense will be expunged.

Please note that there are currently proposed amendments in the Vermont legislature which, if passed, would further restrict the availability of expungement for certain violent sex offenses and offenses against children.

Title 3, Section 164 of the Vermont Statutes, entitled "Adult Court Diversion Project," provides that the attorney general must develop an adult court diversion project in all counties. The program is available to first-time offenders, and it provides that once the offender completes the program, the criminal record may be sealed. The statute is summarized below.

A diversion project established by the attorney general may only accept individuals who have been charged with a criminal offense but have not been adjudicated. Participation in the program is completely voluntary, and all the information gathered on an individual in an adult diversion program is to be kept confidential.

If the individual successfully completes the diversion program, the record may be sealed after two years have passed since the individual's completion of the program. The court must notify the state's attorney general of the potential sealing of the record, and give the attorney general an opportunity to object.

The court will order the record seals if it determines that two years have passed since the individual successfully completed the diversionary program, the individual has not been convicted of another criminal offense in that time, and the individual has been satisfactorily rehabilitated.

Eligibility

In Vermont, the statutes allow for the relief of expungement for adult convictions only in limited circumstances. An individual may have his or her information expunged from the sex offender registry only if the conviction is reversed. Moreover, there is currently a series of proposed amendments being discussed in the Vermont legislature. The new laws, if passed, will further restrict eligibility for expungement in the case of certain sex crimes, such as sexual assault or lewd and lascivious act with a child. In general, first-time offenders for non-felony offenses are the most likely candidates for expungement.

Effect of Expungement

After the court grants an order expunging or sealing a criminal record, the effect is as if the offense never took place. The records may not be accessed by the public, but may be accessed by court order. The individual does not have to acknowledge the existence of the record when replying to any direct inquiry for any purpose. However, the destruction of records for sexual offenses follows special rules. Only in the event a conviction involving a sexual offense is reversed will the record be destroyed.

Expungement for Juveniles

As of January 1st 2009, the Vermont legislature has repealed the previous statute concerning juvenile expungement; specifically, Title 33, section 5538, which dealt with the sealing of records in juvenile proceedings, is no longer valid. This does *not* mean that expungement is no longer available for juvenile offenders. In fact, the individual may presumably still petition for an expungement with the appropriate court, and the court, after a hearing, may still grant the petition. What it does mean, however, is that the Vermont courts are no longer restricted by the now-repealed language in the statute, which implies a wider discretion in whether to grant or deny the expungement. Given the recent law-making activity, it is possible that the legislature may pass new laws relating to expungement in the near future. Therefore, it is worthwhile to carefully watch the Vermont legislature for any possible favorable changes in the law and to contact an attorney in order to effectively take advantage of such changes.

Lesser Remedies

Chapter II, Section 20 of the Vermont Constitution gives the Governor the power to grant pardons for criminal convictions. Ten years must have passed since the date of the individual's conviction before he or she becomes eligible to apply for a pardon. The Governor may request that the Parole Board investigate and advise him or her in the matter.

Vermont Governor's Office contact information:

(802) 828-3333
Governor's Office
109 State Street, Pavilion
Montpelier, VT 05609

Conclusion

In Vermont, the statutes provide for the relief from a criminal record in the form of court order expungement or the judicial sealing of the record. Relief may be available for certain types of criminal conviction. The process of obtaining a court ordered expungement or judicial sealing of records is complex and should not be attempted without the help of an experienced attorney.

As we have said multiple times throughout this book "DO NOT TRY THIS AT HOME." There are tons of pitfalls and perils for those trying to obtain an expungement on their own without the help of an attorney. We've said it before and we'll say it now, *do not try a do it yourself expungement.*

The primary problem is "do it yourselfers" can stir up a long dormant and as of yet un-pursued case. In other words, if you go making haphazard inquiries in the wrong case you can arouse prosecutorial interest and fire up an investigation of you and your case/arrest. Thus, use the resource section of our website at www.ultimatesecondchance.com/resources to help find an attorney in your area.

U.S. VIRGIN ISLANDS

Introduction

In the U.S. Virgin Islands, the statutes provide for the relief from a criminal conviction in the form of expungement for adult offenders and a court order sealing the records for juvenile offenders. An adult offender is entitled to the expungement of his or her record only if he or she is granted a suspended sentence and successfully completes all the terms and conditions of probation.

The Law in the Virgin Islands

Title 5, Section 3711 of the Virgin Islands Code, entitled "Suspension of Sentence and Probation," provides that adult offenders who successfully complete all terms and conditions of court-ordered probation may be eligible to receive an order granting expungement of the findings in the case. The statute is summarized below.

> If the court has found the individual guilty of an offense not involving violence, the court may suspend the sentence and place the individual on probation. The individual may not have been convicted previously of a felony or misdemeanor offense to be eligible to receive a suspended sentence.

If the individual successfully completed all the terms and conditions of the court-ordered probation, the court will discharge the individual without an adjudication of guilt. Once the individual has been discharged, the record of the findings in the case will be expunged.

Title 5, Section 3712 of the Virgin Islands Code, entitled "Probation for Youthful Offenders," provides that individuals under the age of 21 at the time of a criminal offense who successfully complete court-ordered probation may be eligible to receive an order granting the expungement of the entire record of the case. The statute is summarized below.

If an individual is convicted of a criminal offense not punishable by life in prison while he or she is under the age of 21, the court may suspend the sentence and place the individual on probation. The individual may not have been convicted previously of a felony or a misdemeanor punishable by six months or more in jail.

Five years after the individual has completed all the terms and conditions of the court-ordered probation; he or she may petition the court for an order expunging the record of the offense.

If the court finds that the individual has not been convicted of a subsequent criminal offense in those years, the court will enter an order expunging the record.

Title 20, Section 801 of the Virgin Islands Code establishes a point system for motor vehicle offenses. The statute allows for the expungement of certain offenses after the completion of a driver's education course. The statute is summarized below.

Every individual convicted of a motor vehicle offense must be assessed one or more violation points, depending on the nature of the violation. Any individual who collects 12 or more violation points will have his or her driving privileges suspended for six months or more.

If an individual is convicted of a motor vehicle offense that does not involve an accident, he or she may participate in a driver's education course. Once the individual has completed the driver's education course, the moving violation will be expunged from his driving record. This type of expungement is allowed only once every 12 months.

Eligibility

In the Virgin Islands, the statutes provide for the expungement of a criminal record in very limited situations.

Only individuals who were granted a suspended sentence and successfully completed court-ordered probation may petition the court for the expungement of their criminal record. Certain motor vehicle offenses, however, may be expunged after the completion of a driver's education class. The expungement of a motor vehicle offense may be granted only once in a 12-month period. The expungement of any other criminal offense is available to an individual only once in his or her life.

Effect of Expungement

After the court grants a request for expungement, only the finding of guilt in that case is expunged. The statute does not clarify the effect of expunging the finding of guilt alone. After the court enters an order of expungement for a youthful offender under the age of 21 at the time of the offense, the entire record is "obliterated." The individual need not acknowledge the record in response to any direct inquiry for any purpose.

Expungement for Juveniles

Title 5, Section 2531 of the Virgin Islands Code, entitled "Sealing of Records; Expungement," provides that juvenile offenders may petition the court for an order sealing the juvenile records provided they meet certain statutory requirements. The statute is summarized below.

> If an individual was the subject of a juvenile proceeding, he or she may petition the court to vacate its findings and order the sealing of the

record of the proceedings if two years have passed since the individual was finally discharged from custody and he or she has not been convicted of another criminal offense in that time. The court must notify the Attorney General, the Youth Services Administration, and the law enforcement agency with custody of the records.

After the court enters an order sealing the records, it is as if the case never occurred. All records are sealed and unavailable to the public for inspection. Certain governmental and law enforcement agencies may access the sealed records, however, or access to the records may be granted by court order.

If the individual is adjudicated delinquent subsequent to the sealing of the original adjudication record, the order sealing the record of the original offense becomes null.

Title 5, Section 2530 of the Virgin Islands Code provides that if criminal charges brought against a juvenile offender are dismissed, the court may order all fingerprints and photographs of the juvenile destroyed.

Other Remedies

Part II, Section 10 of the Virgin Islands Constitution gives the Governor the power to grant pardons for criminal convictions. The Constitution states the Governor must consult with the Advisory Committee on the Prerogative of Mercy before issuing a pardon. For more information contact the Lieutenant Governor's Office.

Virgin Islands Lieutenant Governor's Office contact information:

(340) 774-2991
Office of the Lieutenant Governor
1131 King Street, Suite 101
Christiansted, St. Croix, VI 00820

Conclusion

In the Virgin Islands, the statutes provide for the relief from a criminal conviction in the form of an order of expungement as well as an order sealing the records of the offense. The process for obtaining relief is complex and should not be attempted without the help of an experienced attorney.

As we have said multiple times throughout this book "DO NOT TRY THIS AT HOME." There are tons of pitfalls and perils for those trying to obtain an expungement on their own without the help of an attorney. We've said it before and we'll say it now, *do not try a do it yourself expungement*.

The primary problem is "do it yourselfers" can stir up a long dormant and as of yet un-pursued case. In other words, if you go making haphazard inquiries in the wrong case you can arouse prosecutorial interest

and fire up an investigation of you and your case/arrest. Thus, use the resource section of our website at www.ultimatesecondchance.com/resources to help find an attorney in your area.

VIRGINIA

Introduction

In Virginia, the statutes provide for relief from a criminal record in the form of expungement. Once an expungement has been ordered by the court, the records are not available for inspection by the general public. The purpose of expungement in Virginia is to protect individuals from the damage that may occur due to an arrest.

The Law in Virginia

Chapter 23.1 of the Virginia Code of Criminal Procedure, entitled the "Expungement of Criminal Records," contains several statutes relating to Expungement proceedings and requirements. Section 19.2-392.2 of the Code of Virginia, entitled "Expungement of Police and Court Records," provides that individuals who are arrested, but not convicted, may petition the court for the expungement of their criminal records. The statute is summarized below.

If an individual was charged with a criminal offense but he or she is later acquitted, the charges are dismissed, or he or she is granted an absolute pardon, the individual may petition the court for an order expunging the record. If an individual was charged with a criminal offense due to the unauthorized use of his identification by another person, he too may petition the court for an order expunging the record.

The petition must include a copy of the warrant or indictment, state the date of arrest and the arresting agency, specifically identify the charge to be expunged, give the date of the final disposition of the charge, and the individual's full name and date of birth. A copy of the petition must be sent to the Attorney for the Commonwealth, who has the opportunity to object to the expungement.

The individual must obtain a set of his or her own fingerprints from a law enforcement agency by providing that agency with a copy of the petition for expungement. The law enforcement agency will send the fingerprints and a copy of the petition to the Central Criminal Records Exchange (CCRE). The CCRE will investigate the individual and send his or her criminal history record information to the court presiding over the expungement proceedings.

After the court has received the criminal history record information from the CCRE, the court will schedule a hearing on the expungement petition. If the court determines that maintaining the record will constitute an injustice to the individual, the court may grant the petition for expungement. If the individual has no previous criminal convictions and the arrest was for a misdemeanor offense, the court must grant the expungement unless the Commonwealth can show good cause why it should not be granted.

Eligibility

In Virginia, the statutes severely limit the availability of expungement. Courts grant expungement only to individuals who were never convicted of a criminal offense. If an individual was charged with a criminal offense of any type, but was never convicted of the offense, he or she is eligible for expungement.

Effect of Expungement

After the court grants expungement, the information in the record may not be released to the public and the record may be released only to law enforcement and government personnel with a valid court order. The individual need not acknowledge the record in response to any direct inquiry for any purpose.

Expungement for Juveniles

Virginia, like many other states, provides greater relief from a criminal record for juvenile offenders. Section 16.1-301 of the Code of Virginia provides that juvenile records are confidential and may not be released to the public. The statute is summarized below.

> Juvenile records must be kept confidential and kept separately from all other criminal records and may not be released to the public unless the record relates to a juvenile over the age of 14 who has been charged with a violent juvenile felony. If a juvenile has been so charged, law enforcement personnel may notify the principal of the school the juvenile attends.

> Juvenile court records not involving violent juvenile felony offenses may be inspected only by the certain governmental and law enforcement agencies.

Section 16.1-307 of the Virginia Code states that records of proceedings against a juvenile in the circuit court are to be treated the same as if the proceedings were conducted in the juvenile court.

Section 16.1-306 of the Virginia Code, entitled "Expungement of Court Records," provides that juvenile records are to be destroyed once the juvenile reaches age 19 and five years have passed since the final adjudication. The statute is summarized below.

> Once a juvenile has reached the age of 19 and five years have passed since the last hearing in any case concerning the juvenile, the record of

the proceedings are to be destroyed. If the juvenile was found guilty of a violent juvenile felony, however, the records may not be destroyed.

If a juvenile was charged with delinquency or a traffic violation and was found innocent of the charges or the charges against him or her were dismissed, he or she may petition the court for the destruction of the records. The Attorney for the Commonwealth will be notified of the request and given a chance to object. Unless the Attorney for the Commonwealth shows good cause why the request should not be granted, the court will order the destruction of the records.

Other Remedies

Article V, Section 12 of the Virginia Constitution gives the Governor the power to grant pardons for criminal convictions. Individuals must wait five years from the completion of their sentences in cases of violent offenses or drug offenses to be eligible to apply for a pardon. Individuals must wait at least three years from the completion of their sentences for non-violent offenses before applying. The Parole Board investigates all applications and makes recommendations to the Governor concerning the course of action to take.

Virginia Pardon Specialist contact information:

(804) 692-0105
Pardon Specialist
Office of the Secretary of the Commonwealth
1111 East Broad St, 4ᵗʰ Floor
Richmond, VA 23219

Conclusion

In Virginia, the statutes provide for relief from a criminal record in the form of an order granting expungement. Only limited types of criminal offenders are eligible to receive an order of expungement. The process for applying for an expungement is complex and should not be attempted without the help of an experienced attorney.

As we have said multiple times throughout this book "DO NOT TRY THIS AT HOME." There are tons of pitfalls and perils for those trying to obtain an expungement on their own without the help of an attorney. We've said it before and we'll say it now, *do not try a do it yourself expungement.*

The primary problem is "do it yourselfers" can stir up a long dormant and as of yet un-pursued case. In other words, if you go making haphazard inquiries in the wrong case you can arouse prosecutorial interest and fire up an investigation of you and your case/arrest. Thus, use the resource section of our website at www.ultimatesecondchance.com/resources to help find an attorney in your area.

WASHINGTON D.C.

Introduction

In late 2006, the Council of the District of Columbia enacted the Criminal Record Sealing Act of 2006. The Act provides for the sealing of criminal records in limited circumstances. The District of Colombia Official Code also contains certain other limited provisions that provide for the expungement of criminal records in certain circumstances.

The Law in Washington D.C.

Section 16-802 of the District of Colombia Official Code, entitled "Sealing of Records on Grounds of Actual Innocence," provides for the sealing of the record on proof of actual innocence. The statute is summarized below.

> If an individual was charged with a criminal offense but never was convicted, he or she may file a motion with the Clerk requesting the records of the proceeding sealed.

> The court will seal the record, if the individual proves that the offense for which he or she was convicted never occurred, or that he or she did not commit the offense. If the court finds that the individual is in fact

innocent of the offense, it will order the records sealed.

Section 16-803 of the District of Colombia Official Code, entitled "Sealing of Public Records in Other Cases," outlines when the court may seal records without proof of actual innocence. The statute is summarized below.

If an individual was arrested or charged with a misdemeanor offense with the exception of a DWI, a sexual offense, or fraud, and did not receive a conviction for the offense, the individual may petition the court to seal the record after two years have passed from the end of the proceedings and he or she has not been arrested or convicted of another offense in that time.

If an individual was arrested or charged with any other offense and he or she did not receive a conviction for the offense, the individual may petition the court to seal the record after five years have passed from the end of the proceedings and he or she has not been arrested or convicted of another offense in that time.

If an individual was convicted of a misdemeanor offense with the exception of DWI, a sexual offense, or fraud, or the individual was convicted of felony for failure to appear, he or she may petition the court to seal the record after ten years have passed from the end of the proceedings and he or she has not been arrested or convicted of another offense in that time.

The court will grant the motion if it finds sealing the record is in the interests of justice. The court will weigh the interests of the individual and the interests of the community in making the decision. The court also will consider the nature and circumstances of the offense and the character of the individual.

Section 16-804 of the District of Columbia Official Code, entitled "Motion the Seal," establishes the procedure and requirements for requesting an order sealing court records of an offense. The statute is summarized below.

An individual must file a motion to seal a criminal record with the court and state the grounds upon which the individual is eligible to have the record sealed. The motion must be accompanied with facts and any evidence in support of the motion. The motion must state all the individual's arrests and convictions. If the motion does not meet all the requirements or the waiting period has not run, the motion will be dismissed.

A copy of the motion must be sent to the prosecutor who may be required by the court to respond to the motion. If it is clear that the individual is ineligible to have the record sealed, the motion will be dismissed. If the motion is not dismissed, the prosecutor must respond. The court will decide whether to hold a hearing. If a hearing is required, the individual may present evidence and the court will grant or deny the motion.

Section 48-904.01 of the District of Columbia Official Code is part of the Controlled Substances Act, and provides that first-time offenders convicted of possession of a controlled substance may apply to the court for an order of expungement. The statute is summarized below.

If an individual is found guilty of the possession of a controlled substance and has not been convicted previously for a violation of the Controlled Substances Act, the court may defer sentencing without entering a judgment of guilt and place the individual on probation. If the individual successfully completes all the terms and conditions of probation, the court will discharge the individual and dismiss the charges against him or her.

After the court has entered an order of dismissal, the individual may apply to the court for an order expunging the records of the offense. The court will hold a hearing and if the court determines that the individual was dismissed and discharged, it will enter the order of expungement.

Section 25-1002 of the District of Columbia Official Code makes it unlawful for individuals under the age of 21 to possess or consume alcohol. Individuals found guilty of falsely representing their ages for the purpose of obtaining alcohol may petition the court for the expungement of the record of the offense. The statute is summarized below.

If an individual is found guilty of falsely representing

his or her age for the purpose of purchasing or consuming alcohol, the Mayor may offer the individual the option of completing a diversionary program in lieu of a formal proceeding.

After six months have passed from the individual's conviction or completion of the diversionary program, he or she may petition the court for an order expunging the record of the offense. The court will enter the order of expungement if the individual has no pending charges against him, and he or she has not been previously convicted of any offense.

Eligibility

In Washington D.C., the statutes allow for individuals who were charged but never convicted of a criminal offense to seek a sealing of their records. Individuals who did receive a conviction are not eligible to seek an order sealing their records until the prescribed waiting period has passed. Most felony convictions may not be sealed. The only felony conviction eligible for sealing is a felony conviction for failure to appear.

Effect of Expungement

After an individual receives an order from the court sealing or expunging a criminal record, the record is retained but is unavailable to the public. If the individual's record is sealed due to actual innocence, further safeguards are placed upon the retained copy of the record, and it may not be examined except upon court order. In any event, once a record is sealed or expunged, it is as if the event never occurred. The individual need not acknowledge the record in response to inquiries. The individual must, however, acknowledge the record if seeking employment with a law enforcement agency.

Set-Aside for Juveniles

Section 24-903 of the District of Columbia Official Code provides sentencing alternatives for youth offenders. The statute is summarized below.

If an individual is arrested and charged as a youth offender, the court may suspend the imposition of a sentence and place the juvenile on probation.

Section 24-906 of the District of Columbia Official Code, entitled "Unconditional Discharge and Set Aside Conviction," provides that once a juvenile offender is discharged from probation pursuant to a youth offender program, the juvenile's conviction automatically is set aside. The statute is summarized below.

Once a youth offender has been discharged, his or her conviction automatically is set aside. The juvenile will receive a certificate acknowledging that the conviction has been set aside. The record of the offense may, however, be used in subsequent proceedings against the juvenile.

Other Remedies

Article IV Section 402 of the Constitution of the District of Columbia is part of the District of Columbia Official Code and gives the Mayor the power to grant pardons for criminal convictions. For more information on applying for a pardon in Washington D.C., contact the Mayor of the District.

Office of General Counsel to the Mayor contact information:

(202) 727-1597
John A. Wilson Building
1350 Pennsylvania Avenue, NW,
Suite 327
Washington, DC 20004

Conclusion

In Washington D.C., the statutes provide for the relief from a criminal record in the form of an expungement or the sealing of a criminal record. The process of applying for expungement or sealing of a record is very complex and should not be attempted without the help of an experienced attorney.

As we have said multiple times throughout this book "DO NOT TRY THIS AT HOME." There are tons of pitfalls and perils for those trying to obtain an expungement or sealing of their record on their own without the help of an attorney. We've said it before and we'll say it now, *do not try a do it yourself expungement.*

The primary problem is "do it yourselfers" can stir up a long dormant and as of yet un-pursued case. In other words, if you go making haphazard inquiries in the wrong case you can arouse prosecutorial interest and fire up an investigation of you and your case/arrest. Thus, use the resource section of our website at www.ultimatesecondchance.com/resources to help find an attorney in your area.

WASHINGTON

Introduction

In Washington, the statutes provide for relief from a criminal record in the form of a judicial sealing. Most types of criminal convictions may be sealed if certain statutory requirements have been met and the conviction has been vacated by the courts.

The Law in Washington

Rule 15 of the Washington Court Rules, entitled "Destruction, Sealing, and Redaction of Court Records," provides a uniform procedure for the destruction, sealing, and redaction of all types of court records. The pertinent parts of the rule are summarized below.

> After an adult or juvenile criminal proceeding, the court, the individual who was the subject of the proceeding, or any other interested person can request a hearing to seal all or part of the records of the proceeding. The individual also may request a hearing for the destruction of the record, but only if express statutory authority allows the destruction of the record. All parties, including any victims, must be notified of the hearing.

At the hearing, if the court determines that the sealing is justified by privacy concerns of the individual that outweigh the public's interest in accessing the record, the court may order all or part of the record sealed. The court may order the destruction of the record only if destruction expressly is allowed by statute.

Chapter 9.94A of the Code of Washington is known as the Sentencing Reform Act of 1981. This Act provides that a conviction may be removed from an individual's criminal history only if it was vacated according to the three following statutes.

Section 9.96.060 of the Washington Code provides that misdemeanor offenses may be vacated and removed from an individual's criminal record. The statute is summarized below.

If an individual was convicted of a misdemeanor or gross misdemeanor and has completed all the terms of the sentence, he or she may apply to the court for an order vacating the record of the conviction. The court will not consider the request if any of the following conditions is present:

1. Criminal charges currently are pending against the individual;

2. The offense was classified as a violent offense;

> 3. The offense was classified as driving under the influence;
>
> 4. The offense was classified as a sexual offense; or
>
> 5. The offense involved domestic violence.

> If the court determines that none of the above prohibitions to vacating a conviction applies to the individual, the court may set aside the guilty verdict or allow the individual to withdraw his or her guilty plea and dismiss the complaint, vacating the judgment and sentence.

Section 9.94A.640 of the Code of Washington, entitled "Vacation of Offender's Record of Conviction," provides that certain Class B and Class C felony convictions may be cleared from an individual's record. The statute is summarized below.

> If an individual has been discharged after the completion of his or her sentence, he or she may apply to the court for an order vacating the record of the conviction. A record may not be vacated if any of the following conditions is present.

> 1. Criminal charges are currently pending against the individual;

2. The offense was classified as a violent offense;

3. The offense involved a crime against persons;

4. The individual received another conviction after his or her discharge;

5. The offense was classified as a Class B felony and less than ten years have passed since the individual was discharged; or

6. The offense was classified as a Class C felony and less than five years have passed since the individual was discharged.

If the court determines that none of the above prohibitions to vacating a conviction applies to the individual, the court may set aside the guilty verdict or allow the individual to withdraw his or her guilty plea and dismiss the complaint, clearing the record of the conviction

Section 9.95.240 of the Code of Washington provides that after an individual successfully completes all the terms and conditions of his or her court-ordered probation, he or she may request that the court vacate the record of conviction. The statute is summarized below.

If an individual successfully completes all the terms and conditions of court-ordered probation, the individual may withdraw his or her guilty plea or request that the court set aside a verdict of guilty and dismiss the charges against him or her.

After the probation period has expired, the individual may apply to the court for an order vacating the record of conviction. A record may not be vacated if any of the following conditions is present:

1. Criminal charges are currently pending against the individual;

2. The offense was classified as a violent offense;

3. The offense involved a crime against persons;

4. The individual received another conviction after his or her discharge;

5. The offense was classified as a Class B felony and less than ten years have passed since the individual was discharged; or

6. The offense was classified as a Class C felony and less than five years have passed since the individual was discharged.

If the court determines that none of the above prohibitions to vacating a conviction applies to the individual, the court may set aside the guilty verdict or allow the individual to withdraw his or her guilty plea and dismiss the complaint, clearing the record of the conviction

Section 10.97.060 of the Code of Washington provides for the deletion of nonconviction data. Nonconviction data consists of all criminal record information that relates to an incident that did not lead to a conviction. The statute is summarized below.

An individual may request that nonconviction data be deleted from his or her criminal record if at least two years have passed since the information was classified as nonconviction data due to a disposition favorable to the individual, or three years have passed since the date the individual was arrested.

The criminal justice agency with custody of the records may refuse to delete the nonconviction data if the individual was granted a deferred disposition, the individual has a prior felony or gross misdemeanor conviction, or the individual was charged with another crime in the two-to three-year waiting period.

Eligibility

In Washington, The Sentencing Reform Act of 1981 establishes that misdemeanor convictions as well as Class B and Class C felony convictions may be removed from an individual's criminal record provided that the individual has fulfilled all the statutory requirements and the court has vacated the conviction. Once a conviction has been vacated by the court, an individual is eligible to request the nonconviction data be removed from his or her record. The court may not vacate convictions for sex offenses or violent offenses, including domestic violence.

Effect of Judicial Sealing

After the court has vacated a criminal conviction, the record of the conviction may be sealed. Once the record is sealed, it may not be examined by the public. Sealed records may be accessed by the public only if the court orders the record unsealed. The record may, however, be available to the court upon appeal or in subsequent criminal proceedings against the individual. Once the record has been sealed, the individual need not acknowledge the conviction in response to any question for any purpose. The court may order the destruction of a criminal record only if expressly permitted by statute. If records are ordered to be destroyed, they are permanently deleted.

Judicial Sealing for Juveniles

Section 13.50.050 of the Code of Washington governs records for juvenile offenders. Juvenile offenders may petition the court to seal the records of a juvenile offense. The statute is summarized below.

> All official juvenile court records are open to public inspection unless they have been ordered sealed by the court. All other records relating to the juvenile are confidential.
>
> If a juvenile has been taken into custody or placed on community supervision, he or she may file a motion with the court requesting that the court vacate the judgment and seal the record.
>
> The court will not grant an order sealing the record unless the following requirements have been met:
>
> 1. If the offense was a Class B offense, the juvenile has resided in the community for a period of at least five years after his or her release from custody or supervision without committing a subsequent offense;
>
> 2. If the offense was a Class C offense, the juvenile has resided in the community for a period of at least two years after

his or her release from custody of supervision without a subsequent offense;

3. If the offense was a gross misdemeanor or misdemeanor, the individual has resided in the community for a period of at least two years without committing a subsequent offense;

4. If the individual was placed on diversion, he or she has resided in the community after his or her release from diversion for a period of at least two years without committing a subsequent offense;

5. No proceedings currently are pending against the juvenile;

6. The juvenile never has been convicted of a Class A offense or a sexual offense; and

7. The juvenile has paid full restitution.

After filing a motion with the court, the juvenile must notify the prosecutor and any interested persons or agencies of the request for the sealing of the record. If the court grants the motion, it will order all the juvenile records regarding the offense to be sealed.

If a juvenile has since reached the age of 18, he or she may request that the court destroy the record of a single referral for diversion. If the court determines that at least two years have passed from the completion of the diversion program, the court will order the record destroyed. An individual who has reached the age of 23 may request that the court destroy all records regarding referrals for diversion.

Other Remedies

Article III, Section 9 of the Washington Constitution gives the Governor the power to grant pardons for criminal convictions. The State Clemency and Pardons Board receive and review all applications. A hearing will be conducted in every case and the Board will make recommendations to the Governor concerning his or her course of action.

Washington Clemency and Pardons Board contact information:

> (360) 902-4111
> State Clemency and Pardons Board
> Office of the Governor
> PO Box 40002
> Olympia, WA 98504

Conclusion

In Washington, the statutes provide relief from a criminal record in the form of a judicial sealing. An individual looking to have his or her record sealed first must have the conviction vacated by the court. The process of obtaining a judicial sealing is complicated and should not be attempted without the help of an experienced attorney.

As we have said multiple times throughout this book "DO NOT TRY THIS AT HOME." There are tons of pitfalls and perils for those trying to obtain an expungement on their own without the help of an attorney. We've said it before and we'll say it now, *do not try a "do it yourself expungement."*

The primary problem is "do it yourselfers" can stir up a long dormant and as of yet un-pursued case. In other words, if you go making haphazard inquiries in the wrong case you can arouse prosecutorial interest and fire up an investigation of you and your case/arrest. Thus, use the resource section of our website at www.ultimatesecondchance.com/resources to help find an attorney in your area.

WEST VIRGINIA

Introduction

In West Virginia, the statutes provide for the relief from a criminal record in the form of expungement. Once an order of expungement has been entered by the court, the records are sealed and unavailable to the general public. The relief of expungement in West Virginia is limited, and individuals with criminal convictions may be eligible to receive an expungement of their record only if they have been pardoned fully and unconditionally by the Governor.

The Law in West Virginia

Section 61-11-25 of the Code of West Virginia provides that individuals who have been found not guilty of an offense for which they were charged or individuals against whom all charges have been dismissed may request a court order expunging their record. The statute is summarized below.

> If an individual was charged with a criminal offense but the charges were dismissed or the individual was found not guilty, he or she may request the court expunge all the records relating to the offense. If an individual has a previous felony conviction, he or she may not

make a request to the court for expungement.

Once 60 days have passed from the order of acquittal or dismissal, the individual may file a motion for expungement with the court. After receiving the motion, the court will set a hearing and notify the prosecuting attorney and the arresting agency, both of which have the opportunity to object to the motion for expungement.

If the court determines no current charges are pending against the individual, the court may grant the motion for expungement and order the records of the offense sealed.

Section 5-1-16a of the Code of West Virginia, entitled "Expungement of a Criminal Record upon a Full and Unconditional Pardon," provides that individuals who have been granted a full, unconditional pardon by the Governor may be eligible to petition the court for an expungement of their records after a number of years. The statute is summarized below.

If an individual has received a full and unconditional pardon from the Governor, he or she may petition the court for an order expunging the record of the conviction. Two years must have passed since the individual received the pardon and at least 20 years must have passed from the date the individual was discharged from his or her sentence before he or she is eligible for expungement. The petition must be sent to the prosecuting attorney, and the individual must publish a notice of the petition as a Class I legal advertisement.

The court will conduct a hearing to verify that the individual actually did receive a pardon and to determine if good cause exists to grant the petition. If the court finds that expungement is appropriate, it will grant the petition and expunge the record. Convictions for first degree murder, treason, kidnapping, or sex offenses may not be expunged.

Section 17C-5-2 of the Code of West Virginia contains provisions for the crime of driving under the influence. The statute provides that individuals under the age of 21 may request the court to expunge the record of such an offense. The statute is summarized below.

If an individual under the age of 21 is caught driving with a blood alcohol concentration of at least .02 but less than .08 for the first time, he or she is guilty of a misdemeanor. The individual may move for a continuance of the proceedings so that he or she may participate in the vehicle test and lock program. If the individual successfully completes the program, the court will dismiss the charges and expunge the record of the offense.

Section 15-2C-5 of the Code of West Virginia, entitled

"Expungement of Registry Listing," provides that registry listings of abuse or neglect may be expunged in cases where the conviction has been vacated or overturned and in cases where the conviction was expunged by the court or the individual was granted executive clemency.

Eligibility

In West Virginia, the statutes provide relief from a criminal record in very limited situations. An individual may be eligible for expungement if he or she was acquitted of the charges against him or her or all the charges against him or her were dismissed by the court. Individuals with actual criminal convictions are only eligible to request an expungement if they have received a full and unconditional pardon from the Governor. Also, individuals under the age of 21 may be eligible to request that the court expunge a first-time offense for driving under the influence, provided they successfully complete a diversionary program.

Effect of Expungement

After the court has entered an expungement order, the proceedings are considered never to have occurred. The individual need not acknowledge the record in response to any direct inquiry for any purpose. After the records are expunged, access to the information may be obtained only with a valid court order.

Expungement for Juveniles

Section 49-5-17 of the Code of West Virginia, entitled "Confidentiality of Juvenile Records," establishes the level of confidentiality granted to juvenile criminal records. For the most part, juvenile records are not available to the public. The statute is summarized below.

> The records of a juvenile proceeding are not open to the public unless disclosure is specifically authorized by statute. Juvenile records are to be disclosed to school officials if the juvenile has been charged with an offense that involves violence against another person, possession of a weapon, or possession or delivery of a controlled substance. If the juvenile case has been transferred to the criminal jurisdiction because the juvenile is being charged as an adult, the records are open to public inspection. The record also may be disclosed pursuant to a valid court order.

Other Remedies

Article VII, Section 11 of the West Virginia Constitution gives the Governor the power to grant pardons for criminal offenses. The Governor will not consider an application for pardon unless it is recommended by the State Parole Board. Once an individual receives a pardon from the Governor, he or she may be eligible to request an expungement for the court in two years.

West Virginia Governor's Office contact information:

(304) 558-2000
Office of General Counsel
Governor's Office
1900 Kanawha, Boulevard, E.
Charleston, WV 25305

Conclusion

In West Virginia, the statutes provide for the relief from a criminal record in the form of expungement or judicial sealing of the record. Expungement is not available for all individuals. The process of obtaining an expungement is complicated and should not be attempted without the help of an experienced attorney.

As we have said multiple times throughout this book "DO NOT TRY THIS AT HOME." There are tons of pitfalls and perils for those trying to obtain an expungement on their own without the help of an attorney. We've said it before and we'll say it now, *do not try a do it yourself expungement.*

The primary problem is "do it yourselfers" can stir up a long dormant and as of yet un-pursued case. In other words, if you go making haphazard inquiries in the wrong case you can arouse prosecutorial interest and fire up an investigation of you and your case/arrest. Thus, use the resource section of our website at www.ultimatesecondchance.com/resources to help find an attorney in your area.

WISCONSIN

Introduction

In Wisconsin, the statutes provide for relief from a criminal record in the form of expungement under very limited circumstances. Adult felony convictions may not be expunged. The only types of criminal convictions that may be expunged are misdemeanor offenses committed by individuals under the age of 21.

The Law in Wisconsin

Section 973.015 of the Wisconsin Code of Criminal Procedure provides the relief of expungement to individuals convicted of a misdemeanor offense while under the age of 21. The statute is summarized below.

> If an individual is under the age of 21 and is convicted of an offense punishable by a maximum of one year or less in jail, the court may order that the record be expunged upon the successful completion of the sentence if the court determines that the individual will benefit, and that society will not be harmed, by the expungement. Once the individual successfully completes his or her sentence, the probationary authority will issue the

individual a certificate of discharge, which will also be forwarded to the court and has the effect of expunging the record.

This section does not apply to records kept regarding convictions for traffic violations.

The court must order the expungement of the record if the individual was under the age of 18 at the time he or she committed the offense, if the offense involved a Class A misdemeanor invasion of privacy.

Section 301.45 of the Wisconsin Statutes, entitled "Sex Offender Registration," provides for the registration requirements and expungement procedures for an individual convicted of a sex offense. The statute is summarized below.

If an individual's information is maintained in the sex offender registry, he or she may request the expungement of that information if his or her conviction was set aside or vacated and if the court has determined that the individual is not required to report such information.

Once the Department of Corrections has received the individual's written request for expungement and a certified copy of the court order vacating or setting aside the conviction, the Department will expunge the information.

Eligibility

In Wisconsin, the statutes provide for the expungement of a criminal conviction only in the conviction was a misdemeanor and the individual was under the age of 21 at the time of the offense. Sex offender registration records may also be expunged, but only in the event an individual's conviction for the sex offense was reversed, vacated, or set aside. The statutes do not address expungement of motor vehicle offenses.

Effect of Expungement

After the court has ordered the expungement of a criminal record, the entire case file must be sealed. Once expunged, the offense is no longer considered a conviction, and it may not be used as evidence in subsequent proceedings.

Expungement for Juveniles

Section 938.355 of the Wisconsin Juvenile Justice Code, entitled "Dispositional Orders," contains a host of information related to juvenile offenses and punishment. The statute also contains information on the expungement of a juvenile record for delinquency. The statute is summarized below.

A juvenile delinquent may petition the court to expunge the record of delinquency once he or she has reached the age of 17. If the court determines that the juvenile has complied with all the terms of his or her sentence; he or she will benefit from the expungement; and society will not be harmed by the expungement, the court will order the records expunged.

The record will also be expunged if it was the juvenile's first adjudication of an Invasion of Privacy offense under section 942.08(2)(b), (c), or (d), provided the terms of the sentence have been complied with.

Lesser Remedies

Article V, Section 6 of the Wisconsin Constitution gives the Governor the power to grant pardons for criminal convictions. Individuals seeking to apply for a pardon from the Governor must typically wait five years after the completion of their sentence before becoming eligible. The individual must publish a notice in the newspaper and give notice to the District Attorney. The Pardon Advisory Board will conduct a hearing and make recommendations to the Governor. A pardon will not expunge a criminal record.

Wisconsin Pardon Advisory Board contact information:

(608) 266-1212
Office of the Governor
Pardon Advisory Board
Room 115 East
State Capitol

P.O. Box 7863
Madison, WI 53707

Conclusion

In Wisconsin, the statutes provide for the relief from a criminal record in the form of a court order granting expungement. Only limited types of criminal convictions may be expunged. The process of obtaining a court ordered expungement is complex and should not be attempted without an experienced attorney.

As we have said multiple times throughout this book, "DO NOT TRY THIS AT HOME." There are tons of pitfalls and perils for those trying to obtain an expungement on their own without the help of an attorney. We've said it before and we'll say it now, *do not try a do it yourself expungement.*

The primary problem is "do it yourselfers" can stir up a long dormant and as of yet un-pursued case. In other words, if you go making haphazard inquiries in the wrong case you can arouse prosecutorial interest and fire up an investigation of you and your case/arrest. Thus, use the resource section of our website at www.ultimatesecondchance.com/resources to help find an attorney in your area.

WYOMING

Introduction

In Wyoming, the statutes provide for relief from a criminal record in the form of a court ordered expungement. Once the court enters an order of expungement, the record is sealed and no longer available for public inspection. The relief of expungement is available only for individuals who were never actually convicted and for first-time offenders with a misdemeanor conviction.

The Law in Wyoming

Section 7-13-1401 of the Wyoming Statutes provides for the relief of expungement for individuals who were arrested or charged with a criminal offense but never convicted of the offense. The statute is summarized below.

> If an individual was arrested or charged with a criminal offense, he or she may petition the court for an order expunging the record if the following conditions have been met:
>
> 1. At least 180 days have passed since the date of arrest or the date the charges were dismissed;
>
> 2. There are no charges currently

pending against the individual;

3. The individual was not placed on probation and granted deferred adjudication or discharge; and

4. One of the following applies:

    1. no conviction resulted from the charge;

    2. no criminal charges were filed in court; or

    3. all proceedings against the individual were dismissed

The individual's petition to the court must be verified and a copy sent to the prosecuting attorney. The prosecuting attorney may file an objection to the petition. If an objection is filed, the court will conduct a hearing on the matter. If the prosecuting attorney does not object, the court may decide whether or not to grant the expungement without conducting a hearing.
If the court determines that the individual is eligible for the relief of expungement, the court will grant an order expunging the record.

Section 7-13-1501 of the Wyoming Statutes provides a mechanism for first-time offenders with misdemeanor convictions to expunge their records and to restore any lost rights to own a firearm. The statute is summarized below.

If an individual plead guilty, *nolo contendre,* or was convicted of a misdemeanor criminal offense, he or she may petition the court for an expungement of the record for the purpose of restoring his or her firearm rights if the following conditions are met:

1. At least one year has passed since the individual completed his or her sentence;

2. The individual has not been convicted of a misdemeanor for which his or her firearm rights have been lost previously; and

3. The misdemeanor offense the individual seeks to have expunged did not involve the use or attempted use of a firearm;

The individual's petition to the court must be verified and a copy must be sent to the prosecuting attorney. The individual must pay $100 when filing the petition with the court. After the prosecuting attorney has received notice of the petition, he or she will notify any victims of the offense. The prosecuting attorney may also file an objection to the petition. After the court has received the petition, it may request a written report concerning the individual's criminal history from the division of criminal investigation. If an objection is filed by the prosecuting attorney, or the individual objects to the criminal history report submitted by the division of criminal investigation, the court will conduct a hearing on the matter. Anyone with relevant information about the individual, including any victims of the offense in question, may speak at the hearing. If no objections are filed, the court may decide to grant the petition for expungement without a hearing. If the court determines the individual is eligible for expungement, and he or she is not a substantial danger to society, the court will grant the order expunging the record.

Eligibility

In Wyoming, the relief of expungement is available only for individuals who did not receive a criminal conviction or first-time offenders who received a misdemeanor conviction. The relief of expungement is only available once to an individual, and it is not available to individuals placed on probation pursuant to deferred adjudication.

Effect of Expungement

In Wyoming, the statutes define expungement as the classification of a criminal record in such a manner as to ensure that it is not available for public inspection. The record is available, however, for use by law enforcement agencies for criminal justice purposes. If an individual received an expungement due to the dismissal of charges, the individual does not have to acknowledge the record in response to a direct inquiry, unless required by law. The prosecuting attorney may appeal any order of expungement granted by the court.

Expungement for Juveniles

Section 14-6-241 of the Wyoming Statutes, entitled "Expungement of Records in Juvenile and Municipal Courts," is part of the Juvenile Justice Act. The statute provides that juvenile delinquents may apply to the court for an order expunging their juvenile record once they have obtained the age of majority.

> If an individual was adjudicated delinquent for anything other than a violent felony, he or she may petition the court for the expungement of his or her juvenile record when he or she becomes of age. If the court determines the individual has not been convicted of a felony since the time of being adjudicated delinquent, that no felony charges are currently pending against the individual, and that the individual has been satisfactorily rehabilitated, the court will order the individual's juvenile record expunged. Once the court orders the records expunged, the effect is as if the juvenile proceedings never took place, and the

individual does not have to acknowledge the record in response to any direct inquiry for any purpose.

Section 14-6-440 of the Wyoming Statutes, entitled "Expungement of Records in Juvenile Court," provides for the expungement of the record of a juvenile adjudicated in need of supervision. The statute is summarized below.

> If an individual was adjudicated in need of supervision as a juvenile, he or she may petition the court for the expungement of his or her record when he or she becomes of age. If the court determines that the individual has not been convicted of a felony since the time of being adjudicated delinquent, that no felony charges are currently pending against the individual, and that the individual has been satisfactorily rehabilitated, the court will order the individual's juvenile record expunged. Once the court orders the records expunged, the effect is as if the juvenile proceedings never took place, and the individual does not have to acknowledge the record in response to any direct inquiry for any purpose.

Lesser Remedies

Section 7-19-109 of the Wyoming Statutes enables an individual to inspect and contest any information contained in his criminal record. The statute is summarized below.

If an individual has a criminal record, he or she has the right to inspect the record for himself or herself. The individual may apply to the court for an order to delete, modify, or supplement any inaccurate information contained in the record.

Article IV, Section 5 of the Wyoming Constitution gives the Governor the power to grant pardons for criminal convictions. An individual must wait ten years since the completion of his or her sentence before becoming eligible to apply for a pardon. Sections 7-13-801 through 7-13-806 of the Wyoming Statutes provide the method for applying to the Governor for a pardon.

Wyoming Governor's contact information:

> (307) 777-7434
> Governor of Wyoming
> Wyoming State Capitol
> Cheyenne, WY 82002

Conclusion

In Wyoming, the statutes allow the relief of expungement in very limited circumstances. The process of obtaining an order of expungement is complex and should not be attempted without the help of an experienced attorney.

As we have said multiple times throughout this book, "DO NOT TRY THIS AT HOME." There are tons of pitfalls and perils for those trying to obtain an expungement on their own without the help of an attorney. We've said it before and we'll say it now, ***do not try a do it yourself expungement***.

The primary problem is "do it yourselfers" can stir up a long dormant and as of yet un-pursued case. In other words, if you go making haphazard inquiries in the wrong case you can arouse prosecutorial interest and fire up an investigation of you and your case/arrest. Thus, use the resource section of our website at www.ultimatesecondchance.com/resources to help find an attorney in your area.

FEDERAL CRIME EXPUNGEMENT

Introduction

Sadly, as of the date of publication, no mechanism for expungement of a Federal charge, arrest or conviction currently exists. However, that may soon change.

Proposed Law

Fortunately, several lawmakers have identified the lack of Federal expungement law as a problem. In response, New York Congressman Charles Rangel has courageously and tenaciously introduced legislation that would make expungement of Federal crimes possible in certain, limited circumstances. Specifically, through numerous congressional sessions, Congressman Rangel has introduced repeatedly the "Second Chance for Ex-Offenders Act," although in each past introduction the bill died. The most recent version was introduced in March 2009.

Congressman Rangel made the following comments on the floor of the House regarding a previous bill and the need to pass it:

Preventing individuals who have served their time in jail from obtaining employment, education and health care only leads to the unfortunate alternative; resort to careers in crime.

Almost all states have in place a system of expunging records or providing a meaningful chance for ex-offenders to rebuild their lives. The federal government has no such system. Therefore, I... the Second Chance Act... which provides that federal ex-offenders have the same second chance as many state offenders.

Federal first time ex-offenders who prove that they have fulfilled all requirements of their sentence, parole and supervised released has been completed; they have obtained a high school or GED equivalency degrees; they have remained free of drug and alcohol dependency; and they have completed a full year of community service, can qualify for re-entry into society and have their records expunged.

It is our view that this legislation should be passed and if you feel likewise, we suggest that you contact your representatives and communicate your thoughts.

Presidential Pardons

In view of the fact that there is no Federal expungement remedy, there is but one other possibility for relief: a Presidential pardon.

As might be expected, obtaining a Presidential pardon is, well, difficult...

It's difficult but not impossible.

In fact, the executive branch maintains an Office of the Pardon Attorney whose job is to take in, review and offer recommendations on applications for Presidential pardons. That office posted the following information and instructions on pardons which we reproduce below:

Information and Instructions on Pardons

Please read carefully before completing the pardon application.

1. Submit the petition to the Office of the Pardon Attorney

All petitions, except petitions relating to military offenses (see paragraph 6 below), should be forwarded to the Office of the Pardon Attorney, Department of Justice, 500 First Street N.W., Suite 400, Washington, D.C. 20530. The completed pardon petition must be entirely legible; therefore, please type or print in ink. The form must be completed fully and accurately in order to be considered. You may attach additional pages and documents to the petition that amplify or clarify your answer to any question.

2. Federal convictions only

Under the Constitution, only federal criminal convictions, such as those obtained in the United States District Courts, may be pardoned by the President. In addition, the President's pardon power extends to convictions obtained in the Superior Court of the District of Columbia and military court-martial proceedings. However, the President cannot pardon a state criminal offense. Accordingly, if you are seeking clemency for a state criminal conviction, you should not complete and submit this petition. Instead, you should contact the Governor or other appropriate authorities of the state where you reside or where the conviction occurred (such as the state board of pardons and paroles) to determine whether any relief is available to you under state law. If you have a federal conviction, information about the conviction may be obtained from the clerk of the federal court where you were convicted.

3. Five-year waiting period required

Under the Department's rules governing petitions for executive clemency, 28 C.F.R. 1.1 et seq., a minimum waiting period of five years after completion of sentence is required before anyone convicted of a federal offense becomes eligible to apply for a presidential pardon. The waiting period, which is designed to afford the petitioner a reasonable period of time in which to demonstrate an ability to lead a responsible, productive and law-abiding life, begins on the date of the petitioner's release from confinement. Alternatively, if the conviction resulted in a sentence other than a term of imprisonment, such as probation or a fine, the waiting period begins on the date of sentencing. In addition, the petitioner should have satisfied the penalty imposed, including all probation, parole, or supervised release. Moreover, the waiting period begins upon release from confinement for your most recent conviction, whether or not this is the offense for which pardon is sought. You may make a written request for a waiver of this requirement. However, waiver of any portion of the waiting period is rarely granted and then only in the most exceptional circumstances. In order to request a waiver, you must complete the pardon application form and submit it with a cover letter explaining why you believe the waiting period should be waived in your case.

4. Reason for seeking pardon

In answering question 20, you should state the specific purpose for which you are seeking pardon and, if applicable, attach any relevant documentary evidence that indicates how a pardon will help you accomplish that purpose (such as citations to applicable provisions of state constitutions, statutes, or regulations, or copies of letters from appropriate officials of administrative agencies, professional associations, licensing authorities, etc.). In addition, you should bear in mind that a presidential pardon is ordinarily a sign of forgiveness and is granted in recognition of the applicant's acceptance of responsibility for the crime and established good conduct for a significant period of time after conviction or release from confinement. A pardon is not a sign of vindication and does not connote or establish innocence. For that reason, when considering the merits of a pardon petition, pardon officials take into account the petitioner's acceptance of responsibility, remorse, and atonement for the offense.

5. Multiple federal convictions

If you have more than one federal conviction, the most recent conviction should be shown in response to question 2 of the petition and the form completed as to that conviction. For all other federal convictions, including convictions by military courts-martial, the information requested in questions 2 through 6 of the petition should be provided on an attachment. Any federal charges not resulting in conviction should be reported in the space provided for prior and subsequent criminal record (question 7).

6. Pardon of a military offense

If you are requesting pardon of a court-martial conviction only, you should submit your completed petition directly to the Secretary of the military department that had original jurisdiction in your case, completing questions 2 through 6 and question 15 of the petition form to show all pertinent information concerning your court-martial trial and conviction. Pardon of a military offense will not change the character of a military discharge. An upgrade or other change to a military discharge may only be accomplished by action of the appropriate military authorities. To apply for a review of a military discharge, you should write to the relevant military branch, at the address listed below:

Army Discharge Review Board
Crystal Mall 4
1941 Jefferson Davis Highway
Arlington, VA 22202-4508

Naval Discharge Review Board
Ballston Tower 2
801 North Randolph Street
Arlington, VA 22203-1989

Air Force Discharge Review Board
1535 Command Drive
Andrews Air Force Base, MD 20331-7002

7. Additional arrest record

In response to question 7, you must disclose any additional arrest or charge by any civilian or military law enforcement authority, including any federal, state, local, or foreign authority, whether it occurred before or after the offense for which you are seeking pardon.

Your answer should list every violation, including traffic violations that resulted in an arrest or criminal charge, such as driving under the influence. Your failure to disclose any such arrest, whether or not it resulted in conviction, may be construed as a falsification of the petition.

8. Credit status and civil lawsuits

In response to question 14, you must list all delinquent credit obligations, whether or not you dispute them. You must also list all civil lawsuits in which you were named as a party, whether as plaintiff or defendant, including bankruptcy proceedings. You must also list all unpaid tax obligations, whether federal, state, or local. You may submit explanatory material in connection with any of these matters (such as an agreed method of payment for indebtedness).

9. Character references

At least three character affidavits must accompany the petition. If you submit more than three, you should designate the three persons whom you consider to be primary references. The affidavit forms provided are preferred. However, letters of recommendation may be substituted if they contain the full name, address, and telephone number of the reference, indicate a knowledge of the offense for which you seek pardon, and bear a notarized signature. Persons related to you by blood or marriage cannot be used as primary character references.

10. Effect of a pardon

While a presidential pardon will restore various rights lost as a result of the pardoned offense and should lessen to some extent the stigma arising from a conviction, it will not erase or expunge the record of your conviction. Therefore, even if you are granted a pardon, you must still disclose your conviction on any form where such information is required, although you may also disclose the fact that you received a pardon. In addition, most civil disabilities attendant upon a federal felony conviction, such as loss of the right to vote and hold state public office, are imposed by state rather than federal law, and also may be removed by state action. Because the federal pardon process is exacting and may be more time-consuming than analogous state procedures, you may wish to consult with the appropriate authorities in the state of your residence regarding the procedures for restoring your state civil rights.

11. Scope of investigation

Pardon officials conduct a very thorough review in determining a petitioner's worthiness for relief. Accordingly, you should be prepared for a detailed inquiry into your personal background and current activities. Among the factors entering into this determination are the nature, seriousness and recentness of the offense, your overall criminal record, any specific hardship you may be suffering because of the conviction, and the nature and extent of your post-conviction involvement in community service, or charitable or other meritorious activities. We encourage you to submit information concerning your community contributions.

12. Exclusive Presidential authority

The power to grant pardons is vested in the President alone. No hearing is held on the pardon application by either the Department of Justice or the White House. You will be notified when a final decision is made on your petition, and there is no appeal from the President's decision to deny a clemency request. The Office of the Pardon Attorney does not disclose information regarding the nature or results of any investigation that may have been undertaken in a particular case, or the exact point in the clemency process at which a particular petition is pending at a given time. As a matter of well-established policy, the specific reasons for the President's decision to grant or deny a petition are generally not disclosed by either the White House or the Department of Justice. In addition, documents reflecting deliberative communications pertaining to presidential decision-making, such as the Department's recommendation to the President in a clemency matter, are confidential and not available under the Freedom of Information Act. If your petition is denied, you may submit a new petition for consideration two years from the date of denial.

Download a Presidential pardon application here:

http://usdoj.gov/pardon/forms/pardon_forms.pdf

OTHER ENGLISH SPEAKING COUNTRIES

Introduction

The concept of expungement is not unique to the United States. Several other English speaking countries throughout the world recognize the benefits of providing relief from a criminal conviction. While every country has its own justice and correctional system, many of the concepts are the same.

CANADA

In Canada, laws grant criminal offenders greater opportunities for rehabilitation and relief from a criminal record than are provided in the United States. The laws provide for the setting aside of a criminal conviction for most types of criminal offenses. If an individual was convicted of a criminal offense under the laws of Canada, he or she may apply to the National Parole Board (NPB) for a pardon.

The pardon process in Canada requires the completion of a number of requirements. First, before becoming eligible to apply for a pardon the individual must have completed his or her sentence and paid all fines assessed to him or her due to the conviction. After completing the sentence, the individual must wait a specified period of time, depending on the nature of the crime. If the individual was convicted of a summary offense (misdemeanor), the individual must wait a period of three years before becoming eligible to apply for a pardon with the NPB. If the individual was convicted of an indictable offense (felony), he or she must wait a period of five years. Individuals sentenced to life in prison are ineligible to apply for a pardon. Once the prescribed waiting period has expired without the individual being charged or convicted of another crime, he or she may apply for a pardon.

Pardon Applications filed with the NPB must include a copy of the individual's criminal record along with a certification that all conditions imposed by the sentence have been fulfilled. The NPB requires a $50 application fee. The Royal Canadian Mounted Police will conduct a general community investigation into the individual's character. The NPB will then make a decision whether to grant the pardon.

Once a pardon has been issued by the NPB, the individual's record is sealed and maintained separately from other records. The record is not destroyed, however, and may be used as evidence in subsequent proceedings. Generally, Canadian pardons for criminal convictions are only recognized within Canada. For more information concerning the pardon process, contact the closest NPB regional office.

National Parole Board national office contact information:

(613) 995-4380
National Parole Board
Ottawa, Ontario
K1A 0R1

THE UNITED KINGDOM

In the United Kingdom, The Rehabilitation Act of 1974 allows some types of criminal convictions to be "spent" or sealed. Convictions are spent automatically with the passage of time. The length of time required for rehabilitation depends on the length of the sentence given for the conviction and not on the type of offense committed. The rehabilitation period also varies depending on whether the individual was under the age of 18 at the time of the offense.

If the individual was sentenced to prison for six months or less, an individual under the age of 18 must wait a period of three and a half years before the conviction is spent. An individual over the age of 18 must wait seven years. If the prison sentence received by the individual was more than six months, but less than two and half years, an individual under the age of 18 must wait five years before the conviction is spent, and an individual 18 or older must wait ten years. For other sentences, such as fines, probation, community service, and so forth, an individual under the age of 18 must wait two and one half years before the conviction is spent, and an individual age 18 or older must wait five years before the sentence is spent.

If an individual is convicted of another offense during the rehabilitation period, neither conviction will be spent until the rehabilitation period for both sentences combined expires. However, minor offenses tried in the Magistrates' Court will not affect the length of rehabilitation. Once the rehabilitation period expires, the conviction remains spent, regardless of any subsequent offenses committed by the individual.

After a conviction becomes spent, the record is not deleted, but remains confidentially in the Police National Computer. Records for certain, minor offenses may be deleted ten years after becoming spent. Once an individual's conviction is spent, he or she need not disclose any information regarding the conviction unless applying for government or agency employment.

AUSTRALIA

In Australia, Part VIIC of the Crimes Act of 1914, entitled "The Spent Conviction Scheme," provides that individuals with certain minor convictions may disregard those convictions after a specified waiting period. If an individual was not sentenced to imprisonment for more than 30 months, he or she may be eligible to disregard his or her conviction under the Spent Conviction Scheme. For adult offenders, the individual must wait ten years from the date of the conviction without receiving a subsequent conviction to be eligible under the Spent Conviction Scheme. Child offenders must wait a period of five years. Sexual offenses are not eligible for disregard under the Spent Conviction Scheme.

After the requisite waiting period, an individual may apply with the Commissioner of the Police for the conviction to be classified as a spent conviction. Once a conviction has been spent, the law prohibits disclosing information concerning the conviction without the consent of the individual. The individual need not acknowledge the existence of the spent conviction in response to any direct inquiry; however, certain government agencies can require disclosure for employment purposes. It is unlawful to disclose a spent conviction for any purpose, and disclosure may result in criminal liability. For more information concerning options under Australian Law, please contact the Department of Justice.

Department of Justice contact information:

Telephone: 03 8684 6600
Corrections Victoria
22/121 Exhibition St.
GPO Box 123A
Melbourne VIC 3001

NEW ZEALAND

In 2004, the New Zealand Parliament passed the Criminal Records (Clean Slate) Act. The purpose of the Act is to allow individuals with certain minor convictions to seal the record of the conviction after a specified crime-free waiting period. To be eligible to seal the record of a criminal offense, the individual must never have received a custodial sentence. In other words, individuals imprisoned for their convictions are not eligible under the Act. Certain other offenses are statutorily exempted from eligibility under the Act, such as sexual offenses. If an individual was convicted of an offense eligible for concealment under the Clean Slate Act, the individual must wait a period of seven years without receiving a subsequent conviction to be individually eligible to conceal his or her conviction under the Act.

To determine eligibility, an individual may request a copy of his or her criminal record from the Privacy Assistant of the Minister of Justice. If an individual meets all of the eligibility requirements under the Criminal Records (Clean Slate) Act, the record automatically is concealed, and the individual does not have to apply for relief. The Ministry of Justice publishes informational pamphlets concerning the effect of the legislation. Pamphlets may be found at local law enforcement offices and courthouses, or an individual may request more information from the Ministry of Justice.

Ministry of Justice contact information:

Telephone: +64-4-918 8800
Ministry of Justice
P O Box 180
Wellington, New Zealand

Conclusion

Regardless of where a conviction originated, the process of clearing a criminal record can be complex. Different countries provide different opportunities and require different standards for eligibility. The process of applying for relief varies dramatically across nations as well. Due to the complexity of legislation regarding the relief from a criminal conviction, it is advisable to retain the services of an attorney familiar with the laws in your region.

As we have said multiple times throughout this book "DO NOT TRY THIS AT HOME." There are tons of pitfalls and perils for those trying to obtain relief from a criminal record on their own without the help of an attorney. We've said it before and we'll say it now, ***do not try a do it yourself method.***

The primary problem is that "do it yourselfers" can stir up a long dormant and as of yet un-pursued case. In other words, if you go making haphazard inquiries in the wrong case, you can arouse prosecutorial interest and fire up an investigation of you and your case/arrest. Thus, use the resource section of our website at www.ultimatesecondchance.com/resources to help find an attorney in your area.

FINDING AN ATTORNEY RIGHT FOR YOU

We have stressed throughout this book that you should not try to obtain an expungement or similar relief without help. Typically this means you should obtain the services of an attorney competent in expungement law.

The primary problem of trying to do it yourself is you can stir up a long dormant and as of yet un-pursued case. In other words, if you go making haphazard inquiries in the wrong case you can arouse prosecutorial interest and fire up an investigation of you and your case/arrest if it did not previously lead to a conviction and the statute of limitations had not run. (Note: The statute of limitation refers to the time after which you cannot be convicted.) In other words, we would not want you to accidently kick a sleeping pit-bull.

Thus, we recommend that you get an attorney who can look at your case without danger.

It is especially important to get an attorney in jurisdictions where the expungement law is vague or non-existent.

As lawyers ourselves, we can say with reasonable certainty that lawyers do their best work in grey areas, in areas of the law where the results of a case are dependent on the quality and connectedness of the attorney.

Additionally, in any circumstance where discretion can enter the process you need an attorney. This means if any discretionary decisions are to be made by the judge, then you need an attorney to serve as your advocate. It could mean the difference between success and failure.

The challenge is finding the right lawyer for you and your case. Here are some suggestions to help you in the process.

1. Interview at least three different attorneys. When you do, evaluate whether:

   a. You're getting an attorney in the same county or city where the arrest took place. That is, get a respected local attorney who regularly practices in the court system that you are about to navigate.

   b. The attorney regularly does expungements.

   c. The fees to do the work are reasonable for the area (you only know this by interviewing at least three attorneys and asking each about their charges).

      i. When asking about the fees make sure you're clear about what the filing fees will be and any other charges.

      ii. From an economic standpoint it is always best to negotiate a flat fee. If possible, pay half upfront and half on completion of the expungement.

  d. Get clear answers for how long the process will take. It's not realistic to expect an exact date but your attorney should be able to give you a range (45 to 60 days) for example.

  e. Your gut is telling you something. In the interview process you'll get a feeling for whether or not you seem to "mesh" with an attorney. If you get a negative or funny vibe, it's probably not a good fit.

2. Here's how to find the attorneys to interview:

  a. Contact the state bar association and ask for a referral to an expungement attorney.

  b. Use a national legal match making service. I've set up a special link for you to use to make this request which is free to you at -- *www.UltimateSecondChance.com/lm*

  c. Each specific judge will have his or her own court coordinator. Call this person and ask which attorneys filed the last one or two expungements in his or her court. As you do this for each court in the city/county where you were arrested, attorney names will start repeating. These are the names to move to the top of your list.

d. As you interview attorneys, ask him or her who else he or she would recommend. You may say something like, "I know you're a great attorney, but if you were trying to get an expungement for yourself who would <u>you</u> use?"

Using this checklist will carry you far on your way to finding an attorney right for you.

ONE LAST THING

We will be making frequent updates to this link www.UltimateSecondChance.com/resources adding new resources for helping you put your past behind you. Check it out…

Now go start your new life…

Made in the USA
Middletown, DE
15 June 2022

67188004R00225